Insights from Spiritual Masters and Guides

Wisdom Quotes from:

Charles Chaplin
Albert Einstein
Jiddu Krishnamurti
Jorge Luis Borges
David Bohm

Table of Contents

INTRODUCTION

History has provided us with a rich amalgamation of geniuses and visionaries whose contributions have enriched our lives and challenged our perceptions of the world. Among these outstanding individuals, we find Charlie Chaplin, Albert Einstein, Jiddu Krishnamurti, Jorge Luis Borges, and David Bohm.

At first glance, these names may seem to belong to completely different fields, but delving into their lives and works, we discover surprising similarities that reveal a common quest for deeper truths. In this text, we will explore those similarities and how these unique personalities viewed life from different angles but converged on certain truths.

Perception of Reality

Both Einstein and Bohm, in the scientific realm, and Krishnamurti, from a philosophical and spiritual perspective, shared a vision of reality as an interconnected and constantly flowing whole. Einstein revolutionized physics with his theory of relativity, which challenged our understanding of the nature of space, time, and gravity. Bohm, on the other hand, developed the theory of the holomovement, which maintains that reality is an indivisible and dynamic totality. Krishnamurti, a prominent philosopher and spiritual teacher, emphasized the importance of freeing ourselves from our perceptual limitations to perceive reality in its entirety.

Nature of the Mind

Borges, the renowned Argentine writer and poet, and Krishnamurti explored the complexity of the human mind. Both questioned the nature of identity and the illusion of a separate "self." Borges, through his stories and essays, revealed how fiction and reality intertwine, challenging our conventional notions of truth. Krishnamurti, on the other hand, emphasized the importance of direct observation and self-inquiry to discover the true nature of the mind and transcend the barriers of conditioned thought.

Critique of Society and The Human Condition

Chaplin, known as a genius of silent film, and Borges, as a writer and social critic, spoke out against the injustice and oppression of society. Through films like "Modern Times," Chaplin exposed social inequalities and the dehumanization of the industrial age, advocating for compassion and empathy as antidotes to the ills of the modern world. Borges, in his literary works, explored themes such as ambiguity, betrayal, and the fragility of human knowledge, leading to a profound reflection on the human condition and the complexity of reality.

Charlie Chaplin, Albert Einstein, Jiddu Krishnamurti, Jorge Luis Borges, and David Bohm, through their visionary perspectives, pointed us towards a new human paradigm in relation to intelligence, thought, and understanding of time. Their approach transcended conventional boundaries and invited us to expand our consciousness, to question our entrenched beliefs, and to explore new ways of perception and understanding.

These contemporary geniuses showed us that intelligence goes beyond intellect, that thought can be a tool of exploration, and that time is a fluid and relative dimension. Their contributions challenge us to broaden our horizons and to open ourselves to new possibilities of knowledge and understanding.

Ultimately, their legacy invites us to reflect on our own relationship with intelligence, thought, and time, and to embrace a more holistic and conscious approach to life. Following the example of Chaplin, Einstein, Krishnamurti, Borges, and Bohm, we can transcend conventional limitations and embrace a broader and more enriching vision of our human potential.

1

Charles Chaplin

About Charlie Chaplin

Charlie Chaplin explored various philosophical aspects throughout his film career. Through his iconic character, "The Tramp," and his movies, he addressed profound themes and reflected on the human condition, society, injustice, and the pursuit of happiness. Some of the philosophical aspects present in his work include the following:

Social criticism: Chaplin used his comedy to critique the social and economic inequalities of his time. His films often portrayed the struggle of ordinary individuals against oppressive forces and unjust systems, emphasizing empathy and human solidarity.

Humanity and compassion: Through his characters and narratives, Chaplin emphasized the importance of compassion and empathy towards others. His films showed individuals' capacity to find kindness in difficult situations and promoted the idea that all human beings deserve dignity and respect.

Critique of industrialism and technology: In movies like "Modern Times," Chaplin explored the dehumanizing effects of industrialization and technology on modern life. He questioned the alienation and mechanization of work, as well as the loss of human connection in an increasingly impersonal society.

Reflections on identity and authenticity: Chaplin addressed the search for identity and authenticity in his films, showing how characters face challenges to maintain their true selves in a world that often imposes masks and social roles.

Irony and paradox: Through his comedic style and slapstick abilities, Chaplin explored the irony and paradox of human existence. His films combined moments of laughter with moments of melancholy and reflection, revealing the complexity of the human experience.

Overall, the philosophical aspect of Chaplin's work focused on universal and timeless themes, addressing fundamental questions of the human condition and promoting values such as equality, compassion, and authenticity.

Dear reader, let me immerse us together in the captivating work of Charlie Chaplin, a cinematic genius who used his art as a powerful tool to awaken consciousness and raise social and human critiques. Through his movies, Chaplin invited us to reflect on the inequalities of his time and to embark on a journey towards empathy and solidarity.

His characters and narratives reminded us of the importance of treating our fellow human beings with humanity and compassion, reminding us that every individual deserves dignity and respect. Chaplin showed us how even in the most challenging situations, it is possible to find kindness and generosity in the human heart.

Furthermore, the cinematic genius delved into the dehumanizing impact of industrialization and technology on modern life. Through films like "Modern Times," he confronted us with the alienation and mechanization of work, as well as the loss of human connection in an increasingly cold and impersonal society.

In his works, Chaplin also explored the search for our identity and authenticity in a world that often imposes masks and social roles on us. He invited us to question our own perceptions and to confront the challenges of staying true to ourselves amidst external pressures.

Through his comedic style and ability to create moments of irony and paradox, Chaplin reminded us of the inherent complexity of human existence. His films took us from laughter to melancholy and reflection, leaving a profound echo in our hearts and minds.

In summary, Chaplin was much more than a brilliant comedian. He was a philosopher of cinema, a master storyteller who invited us to confront fundamental questions about our humanity and to value the principles of equality, compassion, and authenticity. Dear reader, I invite you to delve into his cinematic universe and discover how his films endure over time, touching our souls and awakening our sense of humanity.

Wisdom Quotes by Charlie Chaplin

"LEARN AS IF YOU WERE TO LIVE FOREVER,
AND LIVE AS IF YOU WERE TO DIE TOMORROW"

"NEVER FORGET TO SMILE,
BECAUSE THE DAY YOU DON'T
SMILE,
WILL BE A LOST DAY."

"BEARN AS IF YOU WERE
TO LIVE FOREVER,
AND LIVE AS IF YOU WERE
TO DIE TOMORROW."

"LIFE IS WONDERFUL
IF YOU DON'T FEAR IT."

"TIME IS THE BEST AUTHOR:
IT ALWAYS FINDS
A PERFECT ENDING."

"THERE IS NOTHING PERMANENT
IN THIS WICKED WORLD.
NOT EVEN OUR PROBLEMS."

"AFTER ALL
EVERYTHING IS A
JOKE"

"AS A MAN GROWS OLDER,
HE WANTS TO LIVE DEEPLY.
A FEELING OF SAD DIGNITY
INVADES HIS SOUL,
AND THIS IS FATAL
FOR A COMEDIAN."

"DON'T WAIT FOR YOUR TURN TO SPEAK;
TRULY LISTEN AND YOU'LL BE DIFFERENT."

"Something is as inevitable as death and that is life."

"LAUGH AND THE WORLD
LAUGHS WITH YOU
CRY AND THE WORLD
TURNING ITS BACK
WILL LET YOU CRY."

"Numbers sanctify,
if you kill a few you are a criminal,
if you kill thousands, you are a
hero."

"VIEWED UP CLOSE, LIFE IS A TRAGEDY,
BUT SEEN FROM AFAR, IT LOOKS LIKE A COMEDY."

"THE TRUE MEANING OF THINGS IS
FOUND
IN TRYING TO SAY THE SAME THINGS
IN OTHER WORDS."

"I am at peace with God,
my conflict is with man."

"HAPPINESS... DOES IT EXIST?
WHERE? WHEN I WAS A CHILD,
I COMPLAINED TO MY FATHER BECAUSE I DIDN'T HAVE TOYS
AND HE WOULD POINT TO HIS FOREHEAD WITH HIS INDEX FINGER:
THIS IS THE BEST TOY EVER CREATED.
EVERYTHING IS HERE.
THERE LIES THE SECRET OF OUR HAPPINESS."

"**W**HEN I BEGAN TO LOVE MYSELF,
IT SEEMED TO ME THAT ANGUISH AND EMOTIONAL SUFFERING
ARE JUST WARNING SIGNS THAT I WAS LIVING AGAINST MY OWN TRUTH.
NOWADAYS, I KNOW, IT'S ABOUT 'AUTHENTICITY'."

"MY PAIN MAY BE SOMEONE EL SE S LAUGHTER
BUT LAUGHTER SHOULD NOT BE THE REASON FOR SOMEONE S PAIN."

"**S**MILE EVEN THOUGH YOUR HEART IS ACHING.
SMILE EVEN THOUGH IT'S BREAKING.
EVEN THOUGH THERE ARE CLOUDS IN THE SKY,
YOU'LL GET BY, IF YOU SMILE THROUGH YOUR FEAR AND SORROW.
SMILE AND MAYBE TOMORROW YOU'LL SEE THE SUN SHINING FOR YOU."

"**B**E YOURSELF, AND TRY TO BE HAPPY,
BUT ABOVE ALL, BE YOURSELF."

"**T**HE SADDEST THING I CAN IMAGINE
IS GETTING USED TO LUXURY."

"LIFE IS A PLAY THAT DOESN'T ALLOW REHEARSALS;
SO SING, LAUGH, DANCE, CRY, AND LIVE INTENSELY
EVERY MOMENT OF YOUR LIFE...
BEFORE THE CURTAIN FALLS
AND THE PLAY ENDS WITHOUT APPLAUSE."

My Commentary on Charles Chaplin's Quotes

"Learn as if you were to live forever, and live as if you were to die tomorrow"

– Charles Chaplin

THIS PHRASE RESONATES deeply with me, as it encapsulates a life philosophy that I consider essential.

When I embrace this idea, I find myself in a zone of inner discovery, personal, and also of what surrounds me. I adopt a mindset of continuous observation and learning, seizing every opportunity to acquire, to discover, to open my mind, to explore different perspectives, and to broaden my understanding. I learn from my experiences, from the people I interact with, but above all from my own nature; from nature itself. By adopting this approach of constant learning, I cultivate a curious and open mind, always in search of new knowledge and perspectives.

Furthermore, this phrase also inspires me to fully live each day. It drives me to seize every moment, to savor the small joys, and to nurture my meaningful relationships.

For example, I can imagine a day when I decide to leave behind the usual worries and embrace adventure. I dare to take risks, to follow my passions, and to pursue my dreams without delay.

This phrase is a constant reminder of the importance of balancing learning and action. It's not about acquiring knowledge, but about discovering, marveling. It's a call to live authentically, without postponing the things that really matter and without allowing fear or limitations to stop us in our pursuit of a fulfilling life.

Learning and living in this way allow me to discover the beauty of existence. The importance of living present in each moment. We cannot postpone our happiness or harmony, not even in the interest of achieving our goals; the future is always uncertain but our capacity for the now is always present. Tomorrow is uncertain, and instead of allowing ourselves to be paralyzed by that uncertainty, we must seize each day as if it were the last, this does not imply a waste of energy or an urgency to get what is desired, nor rushing to experience everything, the present state is not a state of euphoria that wants everything, it is an inner state of openness and harmony; a state in which one perceives that everything is how it is happening.

If I were to die tomorrow, I wouldn't rush to seek what I lack, nor to live what I haven't lived, I would simply appreciate more deeply what is next. I would try to die in peace, without euphoria, without haste, without sorrow...

"Never forget to smile, because the day you don't smile will be a lost day"

– Charles Chaplin

THIS PHRASE ALWAYS reminds me of the importance of a positive attitude and the power that a smile holds. A smile can brighten my day and that of others, conveying joy, kindness, and compassion. It's a constant reminder that each day is an opportunity to find something beautiful and to appreciate the little things around us.

Imagine you're having a tough day, full of challenges and setbacks. You feel exhausted and discouraged. However, you decide to remember the importance of smiling and choose to make a small, kind gesture towards a stranger on your way home. You give them a genuine compliment or simply gift them a warm smile. That simple act of kindness not only brightens that person's day but also reminds you that even in the toughest moments, there's always room for kindness and joy. Your smile becomes a little ray of light that brightens your day and helps you overcome any obstacles you encounter.

When I apply this phrase to my life, I realize that a smile can have a profound impact both on myself and those around me. A smile is an expression of joy, gratitude, and openness to the world. It's a manifestation of my inner well-being and can positively influence my mood, even in the most challenging moments. I may face a busy day filled with responsibilities, but I choose to start each morning with a smile on my face, even if I don't feel particularly upbeat.

By smiling, I can positively impact the lives of those around me. A smile can lift people's spirits, convey warmth, and create meaningful connections. I can think of situations where my smile has brightened someone else's day, even when I wasn't feeling particularly well. Perhaps, by crossing paths with a stranger on the street, a friendly smile was enough to brighten their day or create a brief but meaningful moment of human connection.

Every day is an opportunity to find reasons to smile, even in the midst of difficulties. Although challenges may be present, choosing to smile doesn't negate life's problems or vicissitudes; it simply creates an inner capable attitude. No matter what has happened in the past or what is yet to come, I can make each day count by understanding the importance of a serene and loving inner attitude. Each day that I choose to smile, instead of frown, is a day won, full of opportunities to find beauty and happiness in everyday experiences.

"Time is the best author: it always finds a perfect ending."

– Charles Chaplin

THIS PHRASE EVOKES in me a deep reflection on the nature of time. Sometimes, I can feel anxious about the passage of time, worried about the uncertainties of the future or lamenting missed opportunities in the past. However, this phrase reminds me that time has its own rhythm and purpose.

I imagine a scenario where I am immersed in a creative project, such as writing a novel. Initially, I may feel overwhelmed by the task and the expectations it carries. I worry about finding the perfect ending, about tying up all the plotlines and leaving the characters satisfied. But as I progress, I realize that time, not haste, is my ally and teacher in this process.

Time allows me to explore and develop ideas more deeply. It gives me the opportunity to learn and grow as a writer, as I gain experience and skills. Sometimes, time takes me down unexpected paths, presenting me with new challenges and twists in the plot. Although there may be moments of frustration and doubt, I trust that time is weaving the perfect ending in every word I write.

Similarly, in my everyday life, I recognize that time plays a crucial role in shaping my personal story. I may face challenges, go through stages of growth, and undergo important transitions. In those moments, it may be difficult to see how everything connects and has a purpose. But, over time, I can look back and recognize how each experience, even the most difficult ones, has been part of a fully linked process.

For example, I can remember a time when I experienced significant loss in my life. At that moment, it seemed like there was no way to find comfort or overcome the pain. However, over time, I gradually healed and found a new perspective. I could see how that experience had strengthened me, taught me important lessons, and shaped who I am today. Time, in its wisdom, led me to a unique ending, where I found acceptance and inner peace.

In summary, this phrase reminds me that time is a faithful companion on the journey of life. Although there may be moments when I feel impatient or desire to control the outcome, I trust that time always finds a perfect ending. Through its teachings and opportunities, it guides me towards growth, understanding, and resolution. I learn to trust the process and appreciate the beauty of how time weaves each chapter of my personal story.

This phrase has taught me to accept that time is an inevitable and uncontrollable factor in our lives. Sometimes, we may struggle against the flow of time and try to hold onto situations, people, or moments that have already passed. However, time always moves forward and carries us along, even when we wish to stop it.

Time has a special way of giving meaning and purpose to our personal story. As the chapters of our life unfold, time provides us with lessons, experiences, and opportunities for growth. Although we may not always understand the purpose behind certain events or decisions at the moment, over time, we can see how each piece fits into the overall puzzle of our life.

Imagine you are in an unhealthy relationship and cling to it out of fear of loneliness or change. You try to prolong it despite the obvious issues. However, time marches on and eventually, you realize that you can't continue ignoring the signs that this relationship isn't good for you. Eventually, you make the decision to end the relationship, and although it may be painful at the time, over time you realize it was the best thing for your personal growth and emotional well-being. Time allows you to see how that breakup opened new doors for you, provided opportunities to meet wonderful people, and helped you find yourself in ways you never imagined.

"Life is wonderful if you don't fear it"

– Charles Chaplin

THIS PHRASE LEADS me to reflect on the importance of navigating life with courage and not allowing fear to paralyze us.

When I adopt this mindset in my own life, I experience a sense of freedom and openness to the possibilities that life has to offer. Instead of letting fear limit me, facing fear has allowed me to take action and live wonderful experiences. I have met inspiring people, traveled to amazing places, and discovered new passions and talents. Every time I take action despite my own fear, I am surprised by the opportunities and gifts that life presents to me.

Furthermore, when I don't fear life, I can fully enjoy the present moments. I can immerse myself in the beauty of the small details, connect with the people I love, and savor everyday experiences. Fear is a thief of one's consciousness. By freeing ourselves from that fear, we can savor each moment and find wonder in the simplest things.

In summary, this phrase drives me to face life with courage and not let fear paralyze me. By doing so, I can experience the wonder and fullness that life has to offer. I face challenges, discover new opportunities, and find deep gratitude for every experience. Life becomes art, it becomes a canvas full of vibrant colors when I don't fear it and venture to live it with passion and curiosity.

When we live in fear, we close ourselves off, avoid taking risks, and miss out on opportunities that could lead us to wonderful experiences. You realize that life is truly wonderful when you dare to overcome fear and open yourself to the experiences that await you beyond your current perspective.

"At the end of the day, everything is a joke"

– Charles Chaplin

THIS PHRASE REMINDS me that we shouldn't take life too seriously. Sometimes, we worry and stress about things that in hindsight may seem insignificant. It's important to maintain a humorous perspective and find joy in difficult moments.

Imagine you're at work and facing a complicated or stressful situation. Instead of getting carried away by stress and worry, you choose to take a humorous approach. You find a way to laugh at the situation or yourself, which helps alleviate tension and face the challenge in a more relaxed manner. You realize that ultimately, this situation doesn't define your life and that you can find humor even in the toughest moments. In the end, you realize that although challenges are real, you shouldn't let them consume you and that laughter can be a powerful antidote to ease the burden we carry.

"At the end of the day, everything is a joke." In the toughest moments, humor can be a powerful resource to find relief, connection, and joy.

When I apply this mindset in my daily life, I can tackle challenges with a lighter and more flexible attitude. I acknowledge that obstacles and adversities are part of life's journey, but I also understand that it's not necessary to carry them with excessive weight. By allowing myself to find the humorous side of situations, I can release tensions and make room for creative solutions.

For example, when I encounter a complicated problem, I can choose to approach it from a humorous perspective. Instead of stressing out and feeling distressed, I can look for the funny aspect of the situation. Perhaps I'll find an analogy or an unusual approach that helps me solve the problem more effectively. Additionally, sharing a joke or a humorous remark can foster collaboration and strengthen bonds between us.
This attitude is also valuable in personal relationships. Humor can be a powerful tool to ease tensions and improve communication. For instance,

if I have an argument with a loved one, I can choose to use humor to lighten the mood and create a more relaxed atmosphere. A funny comment or an appropriate joke can help reduce conflict and promote a more constructive dialogue.

I can laugh at my own mistakes and not take myself too seriously. This doesn't mean ignoring challenges or minimizing the impact of difficult situations, but rather finding a healthy way to deal with them through humor and acceptance.

In summary, this phrase reminds me that life has a playful and humorous component. By adopting a light-hearted attitude and finding the funny side of situations, I can release tensions, foster creativity, and cultivate deeper connections with others. Humor can be a powerful ally in the pursuit of happiness and well-being, allowing us to find joy even in the toughest moments.

"There is nothing permanent in this wicked world. Not even our troubles."

– Charles Chaplin

THIS PHRASE REMINDS me that life is constantly changing and that no problem or difficulty is eternal. Sometimes, we tend to cling to our problems and feel overwhelmed by them, as if they were a constant burden in our lives. However, this phrase invites me to reflect on the impermanence of difficult situations and to remember that everything in life has a cycle and a transient nature.

Imagine you're going through a tough time in your professional career. You've lost your job and find yourself in a complicated financial situation. At that moment, it may seem like this problem will never go away and that your life will be marked by adversity. But over time, you strive to find new opportunities, learn and grow from that experience, and eventually find a job that brings you stability and satisfaction. You realize that the problems that once seemed insurmountable have become a past part of your life, reminding you that nothing is permanent and that there is always hope and possibility of overcoming difficulties.

The transient nature of things in life and how the problems we face are part of that changing reality. When I apply this perspective to my own life, I can find comfort and hope even in the toughest moments. I recognize that the problems and challenges I face are not permanent, but rather transient and subject to change. This understanding allows me to maintain a resilient mindset and seek solutions rather than getting stuck in despair.

This phrase invites me to value moments of joy and well-being, knowing that they too are temporary. By realizing that everything in life has a cycle, I learn to fully appreciate happy moments and to be aware of their transience. This encourages me to live in the present with gratitude and to enjoy each experience to the fullest.

Understanding impermanence can also foster an attitude of detachment towards material things. I acknowledge that material possessions are ephemeral and cannot provide lasting happiness. Instead of clinging to material possessions as a source of happiness, I seek to cultivate meaningful relationships, enriching experiences, and a deeper sense of purpose.

The ephemeral nature of everything in life, including our problems. By understanding that nothing is permanent, I can maintain a more balanced and resilient perspective in the face of difficulties. This allows me to seek solutions, appreciate moments of happiness, and develop an attitude of detachment towards material things. I accept impermanence as an integral part of existence and find greater peace and clarity on my path.

"As a man grows older,
he wants to live deeply.
A feeling of sad dignity
invades his soul,
and this is fatal
for a comedian."

– Charles Chaplin

THIS PHRASE LEADS me to reflect on human nature and the changes we experience throughout our lives. As we mature and age, our values and priorities may evolve. We may develop a deeper desire to experience a meaningful and authentic life. However, this search for meaning may conflict with certain roles or identities we have adopted.

Imagine someone who has been a successful comedian for many years and has gained recognition for their humor and talent in making others laugh. But as they age, they begin to feel a need for depth and transcendence in their life. Light-hearted humor no longer fully satisfies their inner quest for meaning and purpose. They may feel a dignified sadness in their soul as they realize that their comedic approach is no longer enough to explore the deeper aspects of human existence. This may lead them to explore new forms of artistic expression or embark on a personal journey of self-discovery and spiritual growth.

In my own experience, I have noticed how as I have matured and accumulated life experiences, I have sought greater depth in my interactions and in how I relate to the world. I no longer find satisfaction in the superficial or trivialities, but crave more authentic and meaningful connections.

For example, when I was younger, I could find joy and amusement in superficial situations or in light and shallow humor. However, as I have aged, I have discovered that my appreciation for comedy has evolved.

I now value humor that goes beyond the superficial and has emotional depth and subtle intelligence.

The feeling of "sad dignity" mentioned in the phrase also resonates with me. As one ages, they may experience greater sensitivity and a deeper appreciation of the beauty and complexity of life. One becomes more aware of the fragility of existence and the losses that inevitably accompany the passage of time. This awareness can add a layer of depth and seriousness to the way one experiences the world.

This phrase highlights the emotional transition that occurs as one ages and how it can affect how we live and express ourselves. As we seek a deeper life, this understanding invites us to appreciate the complexities of existence and to find a balance between laughter and a certain reflective depth in life.

"Do not wait for your turn to speak; listen genuinely and you will be different."

— Charles Chaplin

THIS PHRASE HIGHLIGHTS the importance of active and empathetic listening in our interactions with others. Often in conversations, we focus on sharing our own opinions and experiences without truly paying attention to what the other person is saying. However, if we practice genuine listening, we can have a significant impact on our relationships and how others perceive us.

For example, imagine you are participating in a work meeting where ideas and proposals are being discussed. Instead of waiting for your turn to speak and trying to impose your opinions, you decide to listen carefully to your colleagues and give them space to fully express themselves. You focus on understanding their viewpoints and demonstrate genuine interest in what they have to say. As you practice this active listening, others feel valued and respected, fostering an atmosphere of collaboration and trust. Your differentiated listening attitude sets you apart from others and strengthens your interpersonal relationships.

"Do not wait for your turn to speak; listen genuinely and you will be different." This phrase invites me to reflect on the importance of active listening and how it can make a significant difference in our interactions with others.

In my daily life, I have experienced how genuine listening can strengthen my relationships and enrich my experiences. Instead of eagerly waiting for my turn to speak and express my own ideas, I strive to focus on listening attentively and empathetically to the people I interact with. In doing so, I show respect and consideration towards them, and provide a safe space for them to share their thoughts, feelings, and perspectives.

When a friend is going through a difficult time, instead of interrupting with my own experiences or advice, I choose to actively listen and offer my emotional understanding. I give them space to feel heard and understood, without judging or imposing my own opinions. This practice of authentic listening can have a profound impact on their emotional well-being and strengthen our relationship.

Moreover, when we take the time to truly listen to others, we also have the opportunity to learn and grow. We open ourselves up to new perspectives, ideas, and knowledge that we might otherwise have overlooked. By valuing others' experience and wisdom, we enrich our own understanding of the world and become more tolerant and understanding.

By practicing this skill of active listening, we set ourselves apart from those who only wait for their turn to speak. We become someone who cares about others, who shows genuine interest, and who creates a space of trust and respect in our interactions. This attitude can make a significant difference in the quality of our personal and professional relationships.

By practicing active listening, we demonstrate respect, empathy, and consideration towards others, strengthen our relationships, and open ourselves up to new ideas and perspectives. Authentic listening allows us to be different and make a positive difference in the lives of others.

"Something is as inevitable as death, and that is life."

– Charles Chaplin

THIS PHRASE REMINDS us of the inexorable nature of life and death. While death is a fate shared by all, life is a precious and unique gift. It invites us to reflect on the fragility of our existence and to fully appreciate every moment we have.

Imagine you have been facing a serious illness that has threatened your life. As you go through that experience and reflect on the possibility of death, you realize the importance of living fully and valuing each day as a gift. You begin to appreciate the little things in life, to spend time with the people you love, and to pursue your passions with renewed vigor. This phrase reminds you that life, although ephemeral, is an invaluable opportunity to experience, love, and grow.

Life is as unavoidable as death. In my personal experience, I have reflected on the meaning and depth of this statement and how it shapes my perspective on existence.

Life is a journey filled with moments of joy and sadness, successes and failures, loves and farewells. Life encompasses everything, and through all these experiences, life gives us the opportunity to discover who we are, what we value, and what we wish to achieve.

I have experienced moments of overflowing happiness, where I have felt that life is a true blessing. During those times, I have realized the beauty and abundance one can experience in life. On the other hand, I have also faced challenges, losses, and moments of difficulty. These experiences have reminded me of the fragility and impermanence of existence.

The phrase also invites us to value and appreciate every moment of our lives. It reminds us that we cannot take for granted or postpone what truly matters. Every day is an opportunity to be mindful, to seek happiness, to pursue our dreams, and to connect with the people we love.

Moreover, recognizing the inevitability of life urges us to live authentically and meaningfully. It prompts us to make brave decisions, to take risks, and to pursue our passions. It encourages us to embrace uncertainty and to find meaning even in the toughest moments.

In summary, the phrase confronts us with the inescapable reality of life and challenges us to embrace it fully. Life is a fleeting and valuable gift that we must make the most of. Through our experiences, we learn, we grow, and we discover who we are. It invites us to live consciously, appreciate every moment, and seek meaningful purpose.

"Laugh and the world laughs with you; cry and the world, turning its back, will leave you to cry."

– Charles Chaplin

THIS PHRASE HIGHLIGHTS the power of emotions in our interactions with others and how our attitudes can influence how we are perceived and responded to by others. When we show openness and positivity, we generally attract people who share that energy. On the other hand, when we immerse ourselves in sadness and negativity, we may push away those who could offer us support.

For example, imagine you are going through a tough time and find yourself in a stressful situation. You decide to approach it with a positive attitude and find reasons to laugh and maintain an optimistic outlook. As you share your laughter and positive attitude with others, they are drawn to your energy and join you in laughter and joy. Conversely, if you sink into sadness and pessimism, others may find it difficult to connect with you and provide less emotional support. This phrase reminds us that our attitudes and emotions have an impact on our relationships and how we interact with the world around us.

"Laugh and the world laughs with you; cry and the world, turning its back, will leave you to cry." This phrase emphasizes how our approach to our emotions affects how we relate to others and how they relate to us. In my own experience, I have seen how my attitude and emotional expression can influence the dynamics of my interactions with others.

When I choose to laugh and show joy, I often receive a positive response from people around me. Humor and laughter are contagious, and sharing moments of joy can create a positive atmosphere and foster connection with others. For example, in a social gathering, if I start laughing at a joke or a funny situation, others are likely to join in the laughter, creating a cheerful and relaxed atmosphere.

On the other hand, when I am in a more vulnerable emotional state and cry, I have noticed that some people may feel uncomfortable or withdraw. At times, there may be fear or a lack of understanding about how to deal with more intense emotions. People may feel unsure about how to offer support or fear being overwhelmed by others' emotions. In such moments, I may encounter less support or understanding.

However, it is important to note that no phrase should be interpreted as an inflexible rule. Not everyone will react the same way to our emotions, and there are those who will be willing to offer support and comfort when we need it most, even when we are crying. Others' responses may be influenced by various factors, such as their own capacity for empathy and emotional understanding.

Ultimately, what the phrase reminds us of is the importance of sharing our emotions authentically and sincerely. Sometimes we laugh, and other times we cry, and both expressions are valid and natural. We should not suppress our emotions for fear of judgment or lack of support from others. Finding empathetic and understanding people with whom we can share our emotions is crucial for emotional well-being and the development of meaningful relationships.

By choosing to laugh and share moments of joy, we can generate positive connections. However, it is also important to remember that our more vulnerable emotions and tears are equally valid and need to be accepted and understood; they teach us a lot about ourselves. By being authentic in our emotional expressions, we will attract people who truly support and understand us.

"Numbers sanctify, if you kill a few you are a criminal, if you kill thousands, you are a hero."

– Charles Chaplin

THIS PHRASE CONFRONTS us with a harsh reality about society's perception of violence and loss of human lives. It invites us to reflect on how the scale of an event can influence how it is perceived and morally judged.

Imagine that in a conflict, an individual commits a single murder, which is considered a criminal act and is condemned by society. However, in another context, if that same person is part of an army and participates in a war where thousands of people are killed, their role may be considered heroic by some due to the cause or ideal they are fighting for. This phrase confronts us with moral paradox and prompts us to question ethical standards and how we value the loss of human lives.

This phrase, though controversial and provocative, raises deep reflection on how the perception of actions can be influenced by the scale or magnitude of events. In my personal interpretation, this statement suggests that societies often assign different and universally irrational moral assessments.

Taking this idea into account, we could consider a hypothetical example related to history. Imagine someone committing a violent act in a small community, resulting in the deaths of a few individuals. In such a case, society at large would consider that person a criminal and demand justice for their actions. There would be outrage, sadness, and condemnation towards the perpetrator.

However, if we change the scenario and think of a large-scale armed conflict, where thousands of people lose their lives due to military actions, some people may justify those acts or even see them as heroic. In wartime contexts, those who participate in violent actions on behalf of their nation or ideology are sometimes glorified. This may be due to the perception that their sacrifice and actions are justified by a greater good or broader cause.

It is important to note that this interpretation does not mean that we justify or support violence in any circumstance or magnitude. Rather, the phrase invites us to reflect on how society often values and judges human actions relatively and inconsistently.

In my opinion, this underscores the importance of keeping our eyes open beyond laws and norms. A solid ethical perspective does not arise from a text but from conscious beings, deeply aware at every moment. Neither religious justification, legalism, nor even patriotism is the beginning of true universal morality.

Life in its entirety, nature itself, is the beginning and end, and this should be the starting point for any consideration for our decisions and actions.

The phrase raises the concept that the scale of events can influence how certain actions are perceived and morally valued.

"Close up, life is a tragedy, but seen from a distance, it looks like a comedy."

– Charles Chaplin

THIS PHRASE SUGGESTS that the perspective from which we view life can influence how we interpret it. When we get too close to the details and everyday difficulties, we may see life as a tragedy full of challenges and suffering. However, if we adopt a broader and more distant view, we can perceive life as a comedy, full of ironic and humorous situations.

Imagine you are going through a series of unfortunate events on a particular day. You wake up late, stain your shirt just before an important meeting, and then find yourself stuck in traffic. At that moment, life may seem like a tragedy, a succession of frustrating events. However, if you allow yourself to step back from those details and reflect on the bigger picture of your life, you may find humor in the irony of the situation and laugh at yourself. You realize that setbacks are a natural part of life and that, in the long run, those difficult moments can become comedic anecdotes to share with others.

I have found that the way I choose to view and approach events can influence my perception of reality.

When I closely observe the events of my life, especially in challenging or difficult times, I may experience a sense of tragedy. Painful situations, losses, conflicts, or obstacles can overwhelm me and lead me to feel deep sadness or hopelessness. In those moments, life may seem like a stage full of tragedy, where problems and suffering prevail.

However, by stepping back and adopting a broader perspective, I can see life as a comedy in certain aspects. As time goes by, challenges overcome, mistakes made, and difficulties overcome become valuable anecdotes and lessons. Situations that seemed unbearable at the time can become absurd or even humorous as they gain distance and perspective.

An example illustrating this idea is a situation where I made an embarrassing mistake at a public event. At that moment, I felt ashamed and humiliated, considering it a personal tragedy. However, over time, that experience turned into a funny story that I can share with others, and looking back, I can laugh at myself and the situation.

The phrase also invites us to adopt a lighter and more detached attitude towards the challenges and setbacks of life. By understanding that life is a mixture of tragedy and comedy, we can find comfort and relief even in difficult times. The ability to laugh at our circumstances and not take them too seriously helps us maintain a balanced perspective and face challenges with greater resilience.

Although there may be moments of tragedy and suffering, there is also room for humor and lightness. By stepping back and adopting a broader view, we can find comedy in unexpected twists and learn to laugh at ourselves.

"The true meaning of things
is found in trying to say
the same things with other words."

– Charles Chaplin

OUR WORDS AND language are limited and do not fully capture the essence of what we want to communicate. By attempting to express our thoughts and emotions using different words and approaches, we can deepen our understanding and connect more fully with others.

Exploring different approaches, you discover a way to point out and communicate more precisely and deeply what you are trying to express.

Imagine I am trying to describe the beauty of a natural landscape to someone. I can start by using words like "beautiful," "picturesque," or "amazing." While these words convey a certain idea, they may be limited in their ability to fully capture the essence of the landscape, since the word will never be the landscape. However, by seeking other words and forms of expression, I can arrive at more vivid and evocative descriptions.

Poetic descriptions can capture more subtle aspects and convey a deeper sense of beauty and emotion, for example; "The mountains rising on the horizon like silent giants guarding the landscape."

By exploring different words, metaphors, or images, I can discover nuances and richer meanings that enrich my understanding and that of those I am trying to convey it to. This search for more precise and evocative expression allows us to go beyond the surface and dive into the essence and deeper meaning of things.

The phrase invites us to embark on a mental journey towards different forms of expression to approach describing the essence of things. By seeking new words and perspectives, we can discover deeper layers of understanding and appreciation. By using other words to describe something, we expand our ability to convey and understand more fully and enrichingly.

"I am at peace with God, my conflict is with man."

– Charles Chaplin

THIS PHRASE REFLECTS a feeling of harmony and acceptance in the personal relationship with the divine or even with nature, but it also points out that conflicts and tensions often arise in our interactions with other human beings.

For example, you may have a deep spiritual connection and find peace and comfort in your relationship with the divine. However, you may experience disagreements, misunderstandings, or even conflicts with other people in your daily life. This does not necessarily mean that there is a lack of harmony with God, but rather that challenges arise in human interactions. The phrase reminds us that it is important to understand how the mind, thought, and ideas work, as they have the peculiarity of creating fragmentation and division among people.

In my own experience, I have come to understand that my connection with the divine and my relationship with others can be separate and sometimes contradictory issues.

When I say that I am at peace, I am acknowledging my sense of connection and harmony with existence. This connection is not based on religious beliefs or ideals. Being at peace implies feeling an internal tranquility, a trust in the order of the universe, and an acceptance of my place within it.

However, I also acknowledge and accept that my conflict lies in human relationships, in society, in the conditioning that we all carry within us. Interactions with other human beings can be complicated, challenging, and even conflictive. Differences of opinion, disagreements, prejudices, and beliefs often turn into injustices, tensions, conflicts of our daily lives, which can cause emotional or spiritual turbulence.

A personal example that illustrates this statement is when I find myself in disagreement with someone about an important issue. We may have different perspectives and clash in our opinions. At that moment, I may feel emotional tension and internal conflict about how to deal with that situation. On the one hand, I may recall my internal peace and the harmony I feel in my relationship with the divine. On the other hand, I may face the challenge of resolving and addressing human conflict in a respectful and constructive manner.

It is important to note that conflict with man does not necessarily imply a lack of compassion or love towards others. Rather, it is an acknowledgment that human relationships can be complex and that sometimes they require greater awareness to find reconciliation, mutual understanding, and respect.

This phrase reflects a duality in my personal experience. On one hand, I experience peace and connection with the divine, while on the other hand, I recognize the challenges and conflicts inherent in human relationships. Accepting and navigating this duality is an ongoing process that challenges me to seek harmony both in my spiritual connection and in my interactions with others.

"Be yourself,
and strive to be happy,
but above all,
be yourself."

– Charles Chaplin

THIS PHRASE EMPHASIZES the importance of authenticity and staying true to oneself. It encourages the pursuit of happiness while staying grounded in one's own identity and values.

For example, in the pursuit of happiness, one might be tempted to conform to societal norms or expectations. However, this phrase reminds us that true happiness comes from embracing our uniqueness and living according to our own beliefs and passions. By being true to ourselves, we can find deeper and more lasting fulfillment, even if it means going against the grain.

"Be yourself, and strive to be happy, but above all, be yourself." This phrase encapsulates a powerful message of authenticity and the pursuit of happiness based on self-acceptance and self-love. In my experience, I've learned that being true to myself is essential for genuine happiness.

When it says "be yourself," it invites us to embrace our individuality and express our true selves without fear of judgment. It means honoring our values, passions, and dreams and living authentically. By being authentic, we can unlock our true potential and experience fulfillment in life.

Additionally, it highlights the importance of seeking happiness. Each person has their own definition of happiness, and it's essential to pursue what brings us joy and fulfillment. For me, this involves following my passions, nurturing meaningful relationships, and finding balance in life.

However, above all, the phrase emphasizes the importance of being true to oneself. It's about staying true to our values and beliefs, even if it means going against the expectations of others. By being authentic, we can live a life that's true to ourselves and find genuine happiness along the way.

In summary, this phrase reminds us to stay true to ourselves while pursuing happiness and fulfillment. By embracing authenticity, we can lead a more meaningful and satisfying life.

"Happiness... does it exist?
Where?
When I was a child,
I complained to my father because I didn't have toys and he would point to his forehead with his index finger: This is the best toy ever created. Everything is here. There lies the secret of our happiness."

– Charles Chaplin

THIS PHRASE INVITES us to reflect on the true source of happiness, which is not found in material possessions but in our perspective and attitude towards life.

This reflection raises a profound question about the nature of happiness and suggests that its origin lies within ourselves. Perhaps it's like appreciating the beauty of a work of art; a painting may have many characteristics, but the ability to see beauty in it is internal.

In my personal experience, I have discovered that true happiness is not tied to anything external; neither to material possessions nor external circumstances, but it comes from an internal movement or attitude.

I used to associate happiness, even freedom, with having material things. I believed that if I possessed certain objects or resources, we would all be happier.

I have learned that happiness is related to how I perceive and approach life's circumstances. Although we all face challenges and difficult moments, I can choose how to respond to them. By adopting a positive attitude, finding the silver lining in situations, and learning from experiences, I can cultivate happiness even in adverse moments. Happiness is not a final destination but a state of mind and a way of living in each moment.

When I am in the midst of nature, I can be surrounded by natural beauty, such as a mountainous landscape or a sunset on the beach. In those moments, I realize that happiness does not depend on having but on connecting with the greatness and harmony of the world around me. I can experience a profound sense of peace and joy simply by discovering and contemplating the beauty of nature.

The secret to our happiness lies in recognizing that the true source of joy is within ourselves.

"When I began to love myself,
it seemed to me that anguish and emotional suffering are just warning signs that I was living against my own truth. Nowadays, I know, it's about 'authenticity'."

– Charles Chaplin

THIS PHRASE HIGHLIGHTS the importance of loving and accepting ourselves, and how emotional suffering can be a signal that we are living in contradiction with our true identity and values. By embracing our authenticity, we can find greater well-being and fulfillment in life.

When you start to love and accept yourself, you realize that the key to a fulfilling and satisfying life is living according to your own truth and authenticity, which does not depend on traditions, ideals, or beliefs.

In my own experience, I have discovered that self-love and authenticity are essential for finding inner peace and living a fulfilling life.

There was a time in my life when I found myself trapped in a cycle of anguish and emotional suffering. I constantly worried about what others thought of me, sought external approval, and strived to fit into certain standards or expectations. However, there came a moment when I realized that this approach was against my own truth and authenticity.

I began to explore self-love and accept myself as I am, with my strengths and weaknesses. I learned to listen to my inner voice and honor my needs, desires, and values. Instead of seeking external validation, I started to trust my own choices and live in harmony with my true self.

Today, I understand that anguish and emotional suffering are warning signs that indicate we are moving away from our authenticity. Authenticity involves being true to ourselves. Being true to oneself means not accumulating beliefs; beliefs fill us with contradiction and although they are within us, they manipulate us. Embracing our authenticity is not an act of thought; it is an act of silence, of genuine inner peace.

By loving ourselves and living authentically, we access true freedom. By honoring our authenticity, we find greater inner peace and open ourselves to living a full and meaningful life. Authenticity becomes the beacon that guides us towards greater satisfaction and connection with ourselves and the world around us.

"My pain may be someone else's laughter, but laughter should not be the reason for someone's pain."

THIS PHRASE EMPHASIZES the importance of empathy and consideration towards others. It acknowledges that each person has their own experiences and sensitivities, and what causes us pain may bring joy to someone else. It reminds us to be aware of how our actions and words can affect others and to strive not to intentionally cause suffering or pain.

For example, imagine sharing a personal story with a group of friends, unaware that the same story is painful for one of them due to similar past experiences. Although your intention was simply to share and make others laugh, in doing so, you may unintentionally hurt the feelings of that person. The phrase reminds us that we must be careful and respectful towards others, considering how our actions can impact their emotional well-being.

I remember a situation where I shared a personal story with a group of friends. At that moment, I felt vulnerable and hoped to receive understanding and support. However, one of my friends, unaware of the impact it could have on me, made a mocking comment about my experience. Their laughter triggered feelings of pain and frustration in me. I realized that my pain became a source of laughter for them, but that did not justify their laughter becoming the reason for my pain.

From that experience, I learned the importance of being aware of how our words and actions can affect others. I recognized that each person has their own experiences, sensitivities, and perspectives, and it is essential to be respectful and considerate towards them. I understood that laughter can be a form of expression and joy, but it should be exercised with care and empathy, without causing harm or belittling the pain of others.

As I grew in awareness and understanding of others, I made an effort to be more mindful of my words and actions to avoid hurting or belittling someone. I learned to listen to and validate the feelings of others, recognizing that each person has their own emotional burdens, and we should not add more weight to them.

"Smile even though your heart is aching.
Smile even though it's breaking.
Even though there are clouds in the sky,
you'll get by,
if you smile through your fear and sorrow.
Smile and maybe tomorrow you'll see the sun shining
for you."

– Charles Chaplin

THIS INSPIRING PHRASE encourages us to find strength and hope even in difficult times. It reminds us that smiling, despite challenges and emotional pain, can be a source of resilience and open the door to a brighter future. By choosing to smile, even in adverse circumstances, we can maintain a positive attitude and allow light and happiness to find their way to us.

These words highlight the importance of maintaining a positive attitude and persevering despite the difficulties and painful moments that may arise in life.

"Smile even though your heart is aching. Smile even though it's broken. Even when there are clouds in the sky, you'll get by if you smile through fear and sorrow. Smile, and maybe tomorrow you'll see the sun shining for you." This inspiring phrase encourages us to find strength and hope even in the most difficult moments of life. Through my own experience, I have learned that a smile can be a powerful act of resistance and a source of renewed hope.

I remember a time in my life when I faced a series of challenges and adversities. I felt deep sadness and a sense of hopelessness. My heart was filled with pain, and it seemed like gray clouds dominated my emotional sky. However, in the midst of that darkness, I held onto the belief that I could still find the strength to smile.

Despite the pain and sadness I felt, I decided to face each day with a smile on my face. Although I felt broken inside, I chose a positive attitude and a genuine smile. This conscious choice was not easy, as it involved overcoming the fear and emotional pain I was experiencing. However, I discovered that smiling, even when wounded, had a powerful effect on my own attitude and interactions with others.

My smile didn't solve all my problems or instantly make my pain disappear, but it reminded me that there was still beauty and hope in the world. It helped me maintain a positive perspective and find small joys amidst adversity. Furthermore, my smile also had an impact on the people around me. By conveying a positive attitude, I was able to offer a glimpse of light and hope to those going through similar difficulties.

Over time, I discovered that by smiling despite fear and pain, I created a space in my heart to heal and allow the sun to shine again in my life. The smile became a constant reminder of my own strength and ability to overcome challenges. Additionally, it also reminded me that life is a journey full of ups and downs, and that despite the dark clouds, there is always the possibility that light will appear.

The phrase "Smile even though your heart is aching. Smile even though it's broken. Even when there are clouds in the sky, you'll get by if you smile through fear and sorrow. Smile, and maybe tomorrow you'll see the sun shining for you" has reminded me of the importance of maintaining a positive attitude and finding the strength to smile even in the most difficult moments. Through smiling, I have discovered that I can find hope, heal my heart, and remember that there is always light at the end of the tunnel.

"The saddest thing I can imagine is getting used to luxury."

– Charles Chaplin

THE SADDEST THING I can imagine is getting used to luxury. When I think about it, I picture someone who has lost the ability to appreciate the simple and genuine things in life. It's someone who lives immersed in an environment filled with material comforts, surrounded by luxuries and privileges, but has lost the connection with the essence of existence.

I imagine someone who, accustomed to a life of excess and extravagance, no longer finds satisfaction in the small joys and wonders of everyday life. They fail to get excited about a beautiful sunrise, the singing of birds, or the warmth of a genuine smile. The person has become insensitive to gestures of love, spontaneous laughter, and moments of intimacy shared with loved ones.

In this example, I visualize someone who becomes accustomed to living in a luxurious mansion, surrounded by servants and with unlimited access to all imaginable comforts. However, in their busy routine of ostentation, they miss out on the opportunity to enjoy the simple beauty of life, such as walking barefoot on the beach sand, savoring a home-cooked meal prepared with love, or simply contemplating the sparkle of stars on a clear night.

This kind of life devoid of authenticity and appreciation for simple things can lead to an existential emptiness and a sense of loss of meaning. The person finds themselves trapped in a cycle of constant pursuit of more luxury and excess, without finding true happiness or emotional fulfillment.

For me, the saddest thing is imagining that material wealth could overshadow spiritual and emotional wealth. I prefer to find joy and satisfaction in genuine experiences, human connections, and the wonders of nature because in them, I find an authenticity that no material luxury can replace.

This phrase invites us to reflect on the importance of gratitude and appreciation for simple things in life. It points out that when we get used to a luxurious lifestyle and take material comforts for granted, we may lose sight of what is truly valuable and fall into a state of chronic dissatisfaction.

For example, imagine that you have access to great wealth and all the comforts that money can provide. However, over time, you become accustomed to that luxurious life and stop appreciating the simple and genuine things that used to make you happy. You realize that this accustomedness to luxury has led to a feeling of emptiness and discontent. The phrase reminds us that finding joy in the little things and cultivating an attitude of gratitude allows us to fully enjoy life, regardless of material possessions.

"Life is a play
that doesn't allow rehearsals;
so sing, laugh, dance, cry,
and live intensely
every moment of your life...
before the curtain falls
and the play ends
without applause."

— Charles Chaplin

THIS QUOTE EVOKES the idea that life is ephemeral, and we must make the most of it, leaving no room for regrets or missed opportunities.

In my own experience, I have come to understand that life is a precious and limited gift. Each passing day is another page in the book of my existence, a unique opportunity to write my story and experience everything this world has to offer.

Imagine a theater play, where each of us plays a fundamental role. There are no rehearsals, no repeats. We only have one chance to give our best in each scene. It is our responsibility to make each act a special moment, full of passion and authenticity.

I remember one occasion when I was at a concert of my favorite band. The music echoed in the air, the lights danced, and there was an indescribable energy in the place. At that moment, I decided to fully immerse myself in the experience. I sang at the top of my lungs, let the music transport me, jumped and danced without worrying about what others might think. I allowed myself to feel all the emotions that the music stirred in me, from euphoria to nostalgia.

Similarly, I have learned not to fear showing my feelings and emotions in different situations. If I feel joy, I laugh out loud. If something moves me, I don't hold back the tears. If I feel like expressing my love and gratitude towards someone, I do it without reservations. I understand that life is too short to suppress our emotions and act according to others' expectations.

Every moment is an opportunity to create unforgettable memories and enrich our existence. Even in difficult times, I try to find valuable lessons and learn from experiences. The curtain of life will eventually fall for each of us, and when that happens, I want to look back and feel that I have lived fully, without regrets.

This phrase urges us to make the most of every moment of our lives, as life itself is a unique and fleeting experience. It reminds us that there are no second chances or dress rehearsals, so we must be brave and live authentically and passionately, without fear of expressing our emotions and enjoying every moment.

2
Albert Einstein

About Albert Einstein

Albert Einstein was known for his brilliance in the field of physics, but he also had philosophical opinions and reflections on life and society. His philosophy was generally characterized by a combination of rationalism, humanism, and pacifism. Here are some key aspects of Einstein's philosophy:

1. **Relativism:** Einstein is known for his theory of relativity, which revolutionized our understanding of time, space, and gravity. This theory also influenced his broader philosophy, as he argued that reality is relative and depends on the observer. This led Einstein to be critical of absolute truths and to advocate for tolerance and respect for different perspectives.

2. **Intellectual curiosity:** Einstein believed in the importance of curiosity and intellectual exploration. He encouraged free inquiry and freedom of thought as drivers of scientific and social progress. He believed that education should foster curiosity and creativity rather than simply transmitting information.

3. **Humanism:** Einstein had a deep concern for human well-being and individual dignity. He advocated for equality, social justice, and respect for human rights. He believed in the importance of building a society where everyone had the opportunity to develop their potential and lead a meaningful life.

4. **Pacifism and disarmament:** Einstein was a staunch advocate of pacifism and opposed violence and war. He actively participated in pacifist movements and worked on promoting nuclear disarmament. His famous quote "I know not with what weapons World War III will be fought, but

World War IV will be fought with sticks and stones" reflects his desire to avoid destructive armed conflicts.

5. **Spirituality and science:** Although not religious in the traditional sense, Einstein had a spiritual attitude towards the universe. He admired the beauty and order of the cosmos and believed that science and religion could coexist to some extent. However, he rejected dogmatic interpretations of religion that conflicted with scientific evidence.

It is important to note that Einstein's philosophy developed throughout his life and can be found in his writings, correspondence, and public speeches. His opinions can be interpreted in different ways, but overall, Einstein advocated for intellectual freedom, social responsibility, and respect for others.

Albert Einstein emphasized various psychological, social, and individual themes related to human beings and nature. These themes reflected his holistic view of the world and his interest in understanding the complexity of human existence. Some of the highlighted themes include:

1. **Interconnectedness:** Einstein recognized the interconnectedness of all things in the universe. He believed that humans were part of a broader whole and that our actions and choices had consequences beyond ourselves. He advocated for a deep understanding of our relationship with nature and the importance of maintaining a sustainable balance.

2. **Empathy and compassion:** Einstein highlighted the importance of empathy and compassion in human relationships. He believed in the need to understand and appreciate the perspectives and experiences of others. For him, the development of empathy was essential for building a more just and harmonious society.

3. **Social responsibility:** Einstein argued that humans had a responsibility to the society in which they lived. He believed that each individual should actively participate in improving social conditions and fighting against injustice. He advocated for equal opportunities and for the elimination of social disparities.

4. **Creativity and free thinking:** Einstein valued creativity and free thinking as fundamental tools for human progress. He believed in the importance of cultivating imagination and originality in problem-solving and the development of new ideas. He encouraged the liberation from prejudices and preconceived ideas to allow for innovation and advancement.

5. **Pursuit of knowledge and truth:** Einstein emphasized the importance of the pursuit of knowledge and truth as a fundamental goal for human beings. He encouraged questioning and exploring the world around us, and not settling for superficial or dogmatic answers. He believed in the human capacity to understand the universe through science and reason.

These themes reflect Einstein's vision of human nature and our relationship with the world. His approach transcended disciplinary boundaries and encompassed both scientific and philosophical aspects, with the aim of promoting a deeper understanding of existence and the role of human beings in it.

Albert Einstein had opinions and reflections on formal education and advocated for a more holistic and creative approach in the education system. Here are some key aspects of his thinking:

1. **Fostering curiosity and passion for learning:** Einstein believed that the main goal of education should not be simply transmitting information, but awakening and nurturing students' innate curiosity. He advocated for an approach that encouraged students to ask questions, to explore, and to follow their own interests and passions.

2. **Valuing imagination and creativity:** Einstein considered imagination and creativity to be fundamental qualities in the educational process. He believed that creative thinking was essential for addressing life's challenges and encouraged the integration of arts and practical activities in formal education to develop these skills.

3. **Student-centered teaching:** Einstein advocated for a student-centered approach to education, where teachers acted as guides and facilitators of

learning rather than mere transmitters of knowledge. He believed in the importance of adapting teaching to each student's pace and learning style and providing opportunities for independent exploration.

4. Comprehensive education: Einstein did not believe in fragmented education that focused solely on acquiring specialized knowledge. He advocated for a comprehensive education that included both academic and emotional, ethical, and social aspects. He considered the development of social skills and ethical understanding equally important in shaping balanced and responsible individuals.

5. Importance of autonomy and intellectual freedom: Einstein advocated for autonomy and intellectual freedom in education. He believed that students should be encouraged to question, to develop their critical thinking, and to form their own opinions rather than passively accepting information. He advocated for an educational environment that fostered open debate and the exchange of ideas.

In summary, Einstein advocated for an education that cultivated students' curiosity, creativity, and autonomy. He sought a comprehensive education that not only focused on transmitting knowledge but also on developing social and ethical skills. His approach was rooted in the idea that education should be an enriching and liberating process that promoted deep understanding and growth.

Wisdom Quotes by **Albert Einstein**

"THE MIND IS LIKE A PARACHUTE...
IT ONLY WORKS IF WE HAVE IT OPEN."

"We are all very
ignorant.
What happens is that
not all of us ignore the
same things."

"LEARN AS IF YOU WERE
TO LIVE FOREVER,
AND LIVE AS IF YOU WERE
TO DIE TOMORROW."

"THE GREATEST MYSTERY IN THE WORLD
IS THAT IT IS UNDERSTANDABLE."

"IMAGINATION IS
MORE IMPORTANT
THAN KNOWLEDGE."

"EVERYTHING SHOULD BE MADE
AS SIMPLE AS POSSIBLE,
BUT NOT SIMPLER."

"THE SECRET TO CREATIVITY
IS KNOWING HOW TO HIDE
YOUR SOURCES."

"ALL OF SCIENCE IS NOTHING MORE
THAN THE REFINEMENT OF EVERYDAY THINKING."

"EDUCATION IS WHAT REMAINS
AFTER ONE HAS FORGOTTEN
EVERYTHING HE LEARNED IN SCHOOL."

"The important thing
is not to stop questioning."

"INSANITY IS DOING THE SAME THING
OVER AND OVER AGAIN
AND EXPECTING DIFFERENT RESULTS."

"TWO THINGS ARE
INFINITE
HUMAN STUPIDITY AND
THE UNIVERSE
AND I M NOT SURE
ABOUT THE SECOND."

"Not everything that can be counted counts,
and not everything that counts
can be counted."

"THE WHO IS CARELESS WITH THE TRUTH OF SMALL MATTERS
CANNOT BE TRUSTED WITH THE IMPORTANT MATTERS."

"FIRST, YOU HAVE TO LEARN THE RULES
OF THE GAME.
THEN YOU HAVE TO PLAY BETTER THAN
ANYONE ELSE.

"There is a driving force
more powerful than steam,
electricity and atomic energy:
the will."

"MOST OF THE FUNDAMENTAL IDEAS OF SCIENCE
ARE ESSENTIALLY SIMPLE,
AND, AS A RULE,
CAN BE EXPRESSED IN A LANGUAGE
COMPREHENSIBLE TO EVERYONE."

"WE ALL KNOW THAT LIGHT TRAVELS FASTER THAN SOUND.
THAT'S WHY SOME PEOPLE SEEM BRIGHT UNTIL YOU HEAR
THEM SPEAK."

My Commentary on
Albert Einstein's Quotes

"The mind is like a parachute...
It only works if we have it open."

— Albert Einstein

THIS QUOTE INVITES us to reflect on the importance of having an open and receptive mind. It means that just like a parachute, our mind has the potential to take us to new horizons and experiences, but only if we allow ourselves to explore and accept new ideas, perspectives, and knowledge.

In my personal experience, I have found that keeping an open mind has been crucial for my personal and professional growth. For example, I remember when I was faced with a new project at work that was outside of my area of expertise. Instead of rejecting it out of fear of the unknown, I decided to adopt an open mindset and seize the opportunity to learn something new. I immersed myself in research, opened myself to the opinions of my colleagues, and was willing to consider different approaches and solutions. This open-mindedness allowed me to acquire new skills and knowledge, and ultimately achieve success in the project.

Moreover, having an open mind not only involves being willing to learn, but also to question our own beliefs and prejudices. We often cling to preconceived ideas and are closed off to any information that contradicts them. However, by opening our minds and being willing to examine and reevaluate our beliefs, we can expand our understanding of the world and develop a more comprehensive view.

An open mind also allows us to establish connections and collaborate with people from different backgrounds, cultures, and perspectives. By being willing to listen and understand different points of view, we can enrich our own thinking and promote constructive dialogue.

In summary, having an open mind is fundamental to our personal growth and intellectual development. Just like a parachute that unfolds to take us to new horizons, our mind needs to open up to allow us to explore and expand our limits. By maintaining an open mindset, we can learn, grow, and embrace the diversity of the world around us.

"We are all very ignorant.
What happens is that
not all of us ignore the same things."

— Albert Einstein

IN MY JOURNEY through life, I have discovered that each individual, including myself, carries their own universe of ignorances. There is no human being exempt from ignorance, from unanswered questions, and unexplored realms of knowledge. However, it is precisely this diversity of ignorances that enriches us and provides us with the opportunity to learn from each other.

Let us imagine a vast garden where flowers represent the different fields of knowledge. Some have dedicated their lives to the study of exact sciences, unraveling the mysteries of mathematics and physics, while others have found their passion in the arts, exploring the depths of the human soul through music, painting, or poetry. Each flower is a jewel of knowledge, and even though we may approach one, we cannot appreciate the brilliance of them all.

It is in encountering others where our own ignorances surface, and we discover new perspectives. By interacting with people from different paths and experiences, we are confronted with the limitations of our own knowledge. We learn that not all flowers emit the same fragrance or reflect the same colors, but each one has its own unique charm.

The diversity of ignorances teaches us to value the pursuit of knowledge and the importance of intellectual humility. By understanding that we are all immersed in a constant dance of learning, we can open our minds to the exchange of ideas and the discovery of new horizons. Recognizing our ignorance allows us to question, investigate, and seek answers, but it also gives us the opportunity to admire and celebrate the vast areas of knowledge that surround us.

In conclusion, although ignorance may be a veil that envelops humanity, we should not despair, but embrace it with humility and curiosity. By doing so, we open ourselves to the vast universe of knowledge and allow ourselves to learn from the flowers that bloom in the garden of wisdom. On that path, each interaction becomes an opportunity to expand our horizons, and by sharing our own knowledge, illuminate those corners of ignorance that still surround us.

"Imagination is more important than knowledge."

— Albert Einstein

IN THE VAST horizon of the human mind, rises majestically the queen of faculties: imagination. With its ethereal wings and dreamy gaze, it transcends the boundaries of established knowledge and plunges into the ocean of infinite possibilities. In the delicate dance between the real and the fantastical, imagination rises like an incandescent flame that illuminates the paths of creativity and shapes the wonders of the world.

As a child, I remember getting lost in the confines of my own imagination. In the vast universe of my mind, there were no limits or barriers. I immersed myself in unknown worlds, created characters with intertwined stories, and drew landscapes never seen before. In that inner realm, knowledge was merely a starting point, while imagination was the path that took me beyond the known, challenging established laws and opening doors to new realities.

In adolescence, I experienced how imagination became the compass that guided my steps in the search for my identity. Through literature, music, and art, I discovered that true magic lies in the ability to dream and create. While knowledge offered me a panorama of facts and theories, imagination invited me to delve into the world of emotions and perceptions, to explore the depths of my being, and to express in every work of art a part of my essence.

In adulthood, I have realized that imagination is the key that unlocks the doors of innovation and transformation. In a constantly evolving world, where knowledge can quickly become obsolete, it is imagination that drives us to imagine new solutions, to find unexplored paths, and to reinvent the present. While knowledge can provide us with answers, it is imagination that invites us to question and seek new questions, thus expanding the limits of what is possible.

In every poem I write, in every melody I compose, in every brushstroke that caresses the canvas, imagination becomes the muse that whispers in my ear and inspires me to go beyond the conventional. It is in those moments of creative ecstasy where I feel that my spirit merges with the universe and I can grasp glimpses of eternity.

In summary, imagination is a luminous beacon in the vast sea of knowledge. It is the driving force that impels us to explore, to create, and to transcend the limits of the established. Through imagination, we become architects of new worlds, storytellers of extraordinary tales, and artists who shape reality. It is in that realm of the possible where we find the true essence of life and discover that imagination is more than a mere trick of the mind; it is the very soul of our existence.

"The greatest mystery of the world is that it is understandable."

— Albert Einstein

IN MY EAGER days of exploration, I have immersed myself in the tangle of unanswered questions, seeking to unravel the enigmas that populate this vast universe. How is it possible that the cosmos, with its dancing galaxies and its immutable cosmic laws, reveals itself to us in its mathematical and orderly language? What mystery does the canvas of reality hide, allowing us to decipher its secrets and unveil the truths that lie hidden?

I contemplate the majestic flight of birds, the symphony of seasons dancing in harmony, and the intricate connections of nature, and I marvel at the evidence that, despite its grandeur and complexity, I find a common thread that makes them understandable. It is as if the universe itself, in its magnificence, had woven a fabric of meaning that, although at times impenetrable, is designed to be understood by the curious and observant mind.

An example of this understandable mystery lies in the vast realm of science. From the most astonishing discoveries to the subtlest concepts, scientific knowledge unfolds like a map that guides us through the wonders of reality. Quantum physics unravels the secrets of subatomic particles, biology reveals the intricate mechanisms of life, and astronomy allows us to glimpse the farthest corners of the universe. In each of these fields, understanding becomes the key that unlocks hidden secrets and allows us to glimpse the beauty and harmony that underlie the seemingly chaotic.

But beyond the boundaries of science, the understandable mystery is also revealed in human connections. In the depths of relationships, in meaningful glances, and in words that transcend language, we find the ability to understand and be understood. It is in that space of connection and empathy where the greatest mystery of the world unfolds before us, revealing itself as an intimate dance between kindred souls.

In the poetry of everyday life, in shared moments of laughter and tears, in the understanding that unfolds in warm embraces and in gestures of selfless love, I discover that understanding is a golden thread that weaves our lives into a network of meaning and transcendence.

The greatest mystery of the world lies in its capacity to be discovered; understood, in the harmony that underlies its manifestations, and in the symphony that resonates in curious hearts. It is an enigma that invites us to unravel its secrets, to immerse ourselves in the ocean of knowledge, and to embrace the wonder of understanding. In that embrace, the beauty and meaning of the world are revealed before us, and we are privileged witnesses to the eternal dance between mystery and understanding.

"Everything should be made as simple as possible, but not simpler."

— Albert Einstein

IN THE INTRICACIES of complexity, in the twists and turns of knowledge, I find the essence of an eternal truth: simplicity as a luminous beacon in the journey of understanding. In my ceaseless quest for clarity, I have delved into the mazes of knowledge, unraveling threads of ideas and challenging the tangle of intricate existence.

Everything must be simplified, of that I am certain. Like a wordsmith, my task is to refine each idea, stripping it of unnecessary layers and revealing its essential core. Every thought, every concept, must be distilled to its purest form, like the gleam of a star in the deep night.

But here, on the threshold of simplicity, I must remember the delicacy of balance. I cannot succumb to the temptation to simplify beyond necessity, to prune the shoots of understanding until they are naked and devoid of meaning. Simplicity, like a serene river, must flow in harmony with the inherent complexity of the world around me.

An example of this delicate balance is found in the art of writing. Like a pen in hand, I must choose each word carefully, shape the sentences with precision, and guide the reader toward the profound and subtle message that lies at the heart of the text. Every line must be fluid and accessible, yet I cannot forsake the richness of nuances that color the expression. Simplicity, in this context, is a golden thread that weaves the tapestry of understanding without stripping it of its beauty and depth.

Similarly, in everyday life, I find the importance of simplifying without losing sight of the essence. In human relationships, in moments of connection and communication, simplicity is a powerful ally. Honest words, subtle gestures, transcend the barriers of complexity and delve into the core of mutual understanding. But I must remember that each person is a universe of experiences and perspectives, and my task is not to reduce their individuality to a simple formula, but to find the meeting point where simplicity and diversity intertwine in harmony.

In summary, the art of simplification is a delicate dance, where each step requires precision and awareness. As an explorer of understanding, I must strip ideas of their superfluous garments and reveal their naked essence. However, I will always remember that in simplification there is a boundary that must not be crossed, a threshold that separates clarity from superficiality. At that intermediate point, I find the beauty of simplicity that illuminates the path to understanding, but also respects the inherent complexity of existence itself.

"The secret of creativity is knowing how to hide your sources."

— Albert Einstein

I OBSERVE THE great masters, those who have left indelible marks on the canvas of art. I study their strokes, their technique, their words. I immerse myself in their work, letting their voices whisper in my ear and impart their ancient wisdom to me. But here is the secret: it's not about blindly imitating, but about transforming and merging these influences into something new, into something that is a unique manifestation of myself.

Like a magician on the stage of creativity, I learn the tricks and juggling acts of those who came before me. But when I raise the curtain, when I unveil my own act, no one sees the invisible strings guiding my movements. The audience only sees the final result, amazed by the illusion I offer them.

This is how I hide my sources, how I protect the invisible threads that bring my creations to life. It's not an act of deception, but a dance of transformation and reinterpretation. Creativity thrives on influences, experiences, and the vast ocean of knowledge that surrounds us. But it's in the way I amalgamate these sources into myself, in how I metabolize and express them, where authenticity and originality reside.

In conclusion, the secret of creativity lies in knowing how to conceal the sources that inspire us, in turning influences into something of our own and unique. As artists and creators, we are the alchemists of art, the magicians who transform ideas into masterpieces. We hide our sources to reveal the authenticity of our expression, so that our voice resonates in the hearts of those who encounter us.

"The whole of science is nothing more than a refinement of everyday thinking."

— Albert Einstein

ALL SCIENCE, IN its deepest essence, is a reflection of everyday thinking, a dance between the tangible and the abstract. Our being, imbued with curiosity, rises above the mundane and delves into the realm of questions, seeking to unravel the secrets that lie within the universe's depths.

Like an explorer of the invisible, I venture into the confines of the known, challenging the boundaries of the established. My everyday thoughts, those that emerge in the simplest reflections, become the seeds that germinate in the fertile soil of science. I observe the flight of a bird and wonder how it defies gravity; I contemplate the stars in the sky and marvel at their immensity.

Science, on its path to understanding, is a kaleidoscope of ideas that intertwine and succeed each other. As we explore the world around us, our everyday thinking transforms, refines, and purifies. We immerse ourselves in the sea of observation and experimentation, polishing our concepts and forging new perspectives.

An example is glimpsed in the gleam of light, in the enigma of its dual nature. Through observation and reflection, science reveals that light is both particle and wave, challenging our most basic intuition. Everyday thinking teaches us to perceive light as a single entity, but science reveals the complexity of its nature.

Science is the compass that guides us in the labyrinth of knowledge, refining our thoughts and bringing us closer to the truth. Each discovery, each advancement, is a step further in the endless journey towards understanding. Our everyday thinking is the springboard from which we launch ourselves towards the frontiers of the unknown, transforming the ordinary into the extraordinary.

It is through observation, experimentation, and reflection that we transform our ideas into knowledge. Science is the path that allows us to transcend our limitations and explore the depths of the universe, illuminating our understanding and eliciting new questions.

"Education is what remains after one has forgotten everything he learned in school."

»

— Albert Einstein

"EDUCATION IS WHAT remains after we forget everything we learned in school" is a powerful reminder that true education goes beyond academic knowledge and concepts taught in the school environment.

While formal education provides a solid foundation of knowledge and skills, its true value lies in the ability to apply and adapt that knowledge in everyday life. It's true that over time, we may forget specific details and theories we learned in school, but what remains are the fundamentals, critical thinking skills, and analytical approach we developed through our education.

Education, in its broadest sense, encompasses inner learning, a type of knowledge that cannot be conveyed by others, like information or news, but that is fundamental for continuous personal development throughout life.

Imagine you learned to use a specific application or software program during your school education. After a while, you may forget the specific details of how to use that particular application. However, what really matters is that you have developed the ability to learn and adapt to new technologies. Your education has provided you with the groundwork to understand the underlying concepts and logic behind the functioning of computer applications in general. This allows you to quickly learn new tools and adapt to technological advances as they arise.

Education also reflects in the ability to apply the ethical and moral principles we have learned. Beyond mathematical formulas or historical facts, education helps us develop a sense of responsibility, empathy, and respect for others. These fundamental values guide us in decision-making and in how we interact with the world around us.

True education goes beyond the acquisition of specific knowledge or information and focuses on the development of awareness and intelligence, skills, values, and the ability to adapt to a constantly changing world. Education is a self-process, not just an external contact. We have much to learn from our own being, for which we need conscious self-observation of our own existence and our reactions or actions.

"The important thing is not to stop asking questions."

— Albert Einstein

IN MY CONSTANT quest for knowledge, I have discovered that the key to expanding my understanding of the world lies in never ceasing to ask questions. Every answer I find is just a piece of a larger puzzle, revealing new mysteries and possibilities.

Imagine walking along an endless path, surrounded by a fog of uncertainty. As you progress, you encounter crossings and detours, realizing that each corner hides a question waiting to be asked. What is the purpose of my existence? How can I achieve fulfillment in my life? What lies beyond what my eyes can see?

Each question is like a key that unlocks a door to a vast world of knowledge and understanding. As I seek answers, I discover that some questions can lead me down unexpected paths, challenging my beliefs and expanding my perspective. At times, the answers I find generate new questions, creating an infinite cycle of inquiry and learning.

An example of this tireless pursuit of answers lies in my fascination with nature. I observe the leaves of a tree and wonder how they perform photosynthesis. I explore the movements of the stars in the sky and marvel at the immensity of the universe. Every discovery I make drives me to delve even deeper, to unravel the mysteries hidden beneath the surface of apparent simplicity.

Ultimately, I have come to understand that there is no endpoint in this quest for knowledge. The true value lies in the process itself, in the passion for discovery, and in the humility to recognize that there is always more to learn. By keeping the flame of curiosity alive, I continue to open doors to a world of possibilities and personal growth.

Each question invites us to explore new territories of knowledge. It is in that constant questioning where we find enrichment and expansion of our minds.

"I never think about the future. It arrives too soon."

— Albert Einstein

I RECALL A particular episode that helped me understand the true meaning of this phrase. Some years ago, I was planning a dream vacation to an exotic destination. I researched all the details, booked flights and accommodation, and began dreaming about all the exciting experiences I would have. But while I was busy with those preparations, I neglected what was happening in my life at that moment.

One day, while absorbed in planning my vacation, I received a call from a close friend who was going through a tough time. He desperately needed someone to listen to him and support him. At that moment, I realized that I was letting the present opportunities in my life slip away by being so focused on the future. I missed moments of genuine connection and personal growth because of my constant anticipation.

That's when I decided to make a change. I started practicing mindfulness and being aware of each present moment. I learned to appreciate the little things in life and cultivate meaningful relationships in the here and now. Although I still make plans and set goals, I make sure not to lose sight of the current moment and to enjoy every step of the way.

So, for me, never thinking about the future doesn't mean completely abandoning planning or goal-setting. Rather, it's about finding a balance between preparation and appreciation of the present. The future will arrive when it arrives, but I don't want my anticipatory worries to prevent me from fully living in the now.

"Two things are infinite: human stupidity and the universe; and I'm not sure about the second."

— Albert Einstein

WHEN ALBERT EINSTEIN uttered that famous phrase, 'Only two things are infinite, the universe and human stupidity, and I'm not sure about the former.' he surely didn't imagine the significance it would have in popular culture and our everyday reflections. As a curious person thirsty for knowledge, I have taken the time to reflect on these words and try to understand their deeper meaning.

Firstly, Einstein's assertion about human stupidity as something infinite may seem disheartening. However, throughout my life, I have witnessed numerous examples that support this claim. From impulsive and irrational actions to decisions that defy common sense, human stupidity seems to manifest everywhere. A concrete example could be the moment when someone decides to jump off a bridge to get a fleeting dose of adrenaline.

On the other hand, when Einstein mentions that he's not sure about the second, the universe, he raises a fascinating doubt. The universe is vast and mysterious, and although we have made significant advances in our scientific knowledge, there is still much to discover. In this sense, the universe can be considered a metaphor for the unknown and the unexplored. Just as the universe expands into the unknown, so does our understanding and our ability to comprehend it. Just as outer space remains an enigma in many respects, so too are the depths of our own existence and the mysteries of the human mind.

When Einstein mentioned human stupidity as something infinite, I could understand his perspective. Throughout my life, I have witnessed countless examples that support this assertion. Stupidity manifests in the irrational decisions we make and the senseless actions that lead us to unfavorable outcomes. It's as if our own capacity for reasoning gets lost in an endless abyss. Imagine a turbulent river flowing without control, sweeping away the hopes and dreams of those who cannot overcome their own limitations. That is human stupidity, a current that drags us toward ignorance and prevents us from reaching our true potential.

Ultimately, Einstein's phrase invites us to reflect on our limitations and our capabilities as human beings. Human stupidity may be an undeniable reality, but we are also capable of great achievements and discoveries. Perhaps, by acknowledging our own stupidity, we can be more humble and open to the possibility of learning and growing. Perhaps, by embracing the uncertainty of the universe, we can marvel at the beauty and mystery that surrounds us.

Although stupidity may seem disheartening, we must also remember that we are capable of great feats and that there is always more to discover in the vast universe around us."

"Not everything that can be counted counts, and not everything that counts can be counted."

— Albert Einstein

THE INTRIGUING AND profound phrase "Not everything that counts can be counted, and not everything that can be counted counts" has captured my attention and sparked deep reflection in my mind.

In a world that values numbers and quantitative measurements as indicators of success and worth, this phrase presents an alternative and thought-provoking perspective. Sometimes, we take for granted that only what can be measured and numerically expressed is what truly matters. However, this statement challenges that assumption and suggests that there are more subtle and significant aspects of life that cannot be reduced to figures.

A practical example of this could be love. Love is an immense and not exclusively human experience that cannot be quantified in terms of units or numbers. We cannot measure love in kilograms or meters. We cannot assign it a specific number to determine its authenticity or its worth. However, love is the most powerful and transformative force in life. It is what drives us to connect with others, to care for and understand each other, and even though it cannot be quantified, love may well be what drives the universe itself.

On the other hand, the second part of the phrase also invites us to reflect. Sometimes, we become so obsessed with quantifying things that we lose sight of the truth. We focus on collecting data and statistics without considering whether those data truly represent the essence of what we are measuring. For example, in the field of education, it is common to use standardized tests to measure student performance. However, these tests do not capture the entirety of students' skills and abilities. Even measuring creativity, empathy, or the ability to solve problems innovatively falls short of measuring the ineffable qualities that make a child, a person, or even a small pet, into something immense.

In summary, the phrase "Not everything that counts can be counted, and not everything that can be counted counts" urges us to look beyond measurements and figures in our search for meaning and worth. It reminds us that there are aspects of life that are difficult to measure and cannot be reduced to numbers, but are still essential and fundamental. By considering this, we can adopt a broader perspective and understand that what truly matters goes beyond what can be quantified.

"**I**nsanity is doing the same thing over and over again and expecting different results."

— Albert Einstein

PEOPLE OFTEN CLING to repetitive patterns and behaviors, hoping that somehow the results will magically change.

When someone repeats an action over and over again but expects a different outcome, they are showing a lack of attention to their own actions. Imagine a person who constantly seeks romantic relationships with unsuitable partners. Despite repeated disappointments and mismatches, they continue to choose the same type of people hoping that somehow, next time will be different. This is a clear example of the insanity referred to in the phrase. The person clings to a pattern that has proven to be ineffective but still expects a different outcome without making any changes or introspection.

The most common practical example of this phrase is found in the workplace. Often, organizations and individuals face challenges and obstacles that require new and creative solutions. However, some people or companies may get stuck in a routine where they simply repeat the same methods and approaches, even when the results are not as expected. This may be due to the comfort of the familiar or fear of change. For example, imagine a business that has been using the same marketing strategies for years, even though sales are stagnant or declining. If they continue to do the same without seeking new ideas or approaches, it is unlikely that the results will improve. The lack of adaptation and experimentation only perpetuates the insanity described in the phrase.

The key to breaking this cycle of insanity is the ability to recognize the need for change and be willing to try new ways of doing things. To do this, it is essential to learn from past experiences and seek alternative solutions. Instead of repeating ineffective patterns, it is necessary to explore different approaches, think creatively, and adapt to changing circumstances. Only through experimentation and flexibility can we hope to achieve different results.

In summary, the phrase "Insanity is doing the same thing over and over again, expecting different results" is a powerful observation about the importance of learning and adaptability in our lives. A practical example can be found in personal relationships or in the workplace, where people or organizations get stuck in repetitive patterns without achieving different results. Only by recognizing the need for change, learning from past experiences, and being willing to try new ways of doing things can we break free from insanity and seek more positive and satisfying outcomes.

"First, you have to learn the rules of the game. Then you have to play better than anyone else."

— Albert Einstein

WHEN IMMERSING OURSELVES in any discipline or field of study, it's crucial to understand the rules and basic fundamentals that govern it. This applies to any activity, including life itself.

Imagine you're passionate about the art of photography, but you have no previous knowledge of composition, lighting, and focusing techniques. In this situation, it would be challenging to achieve exceptional results. However, by learning the rules and fundamental concepts of photography, such as the rule of thirds or proper use of light, you can begin to take higher quality photographs with artistic expression. It's through mastering these rules that your essence and being find their way into certain creative spheres.

Before one can innovate and excel, it's essential to comprehend certain principles that govern an activity or field of knowledge. However, the true challenge lies in going beyond merely learning the rules and maps because becoming an outstanding player requires the innovation that only comes from the individual's lived experiences.

When mentioning the need to learn the rules of the game, it refers to understanding and mastering the fundamentals, rules, and essential strategies that govern a particular field of action. Imagine a chess player aspiring to be a master. Before facing experienced players and excelling in tournaments, they must familiarize themselves with the rules of chess, learn various openings, understand tactics, and study games of prominent chess players.

The knowledge of the rules of the game provides understanding but not experience; it sets the fundamental framework for one to move beyond those boundaries. We can cite Picasso and many others who, although mastering traditional painting techniques, were able to expand the space of consciousness that at the beginning of the 20th century limited us to certain styles and interpretations of objects and subjects.

Once we've acquired knowledge of the rules and basic skills, it's time to differentiate ourselves and stand out in the chosen field. This requires dedication, practice, and a constant focus on improving and surpassing established standards.

In a way, one must learn, one must forget, and finally, one can create.

"There is a driving force more powerful than steam, electricity and atomic energy: the will"

— Albert Einstein

WILLPOWER, THAT INTERNAL and powerful force that arises from our desires and determination, has the potential to propel us beyond physical limitations and overcome any obstacle that stands in our way. It is a driving energy that urges us to act, to persevere, and to achieve significant accomplishments. While steam, electricity, and atomic energy are powerful forms of energy that have transformed our world, willpower is an even more potent force because it comes from our inner being, from our aspirations, and from our ability to overcome adversity.

A practical example of this assertion can be found in the stories of many successful and entrepreneurial individuals who have achieved great things through their unyielding willpower. Let's take the example of Thomas Edison, a prolific inventor whose determination and willpower allowed him to overcome countless failures before inventing the incandescent light bulb. Despite facing multiple setbacks and difficulties along the way, Edison never gave up. His will to turn his vision into reality led him to conduct countless experiments and to persevere despite obstacles. His famous quote, "I have not failed. I've just found 10,000 ways that won't work," illustrates the powerful force of willpower and how it can lead to success even in the most challenging circumstances.

Willpower also shines in the sports arena, where athletes surpass their own limits and achieve outstanding performance. Think of the Olympic athletes who dedicate years of training and sacrifice to compete in the Olympic Games. Their willpower to overcome difficulties, to push through despite injuries, and to maintain their focus on excellence drives them to achieve extraordinary results. Their internal motivation and willpower to give their best propel them to reach outstanding marks and medals in the world's most prestigious sporting event.

In summary, the phrase "There is a driving force more powerful than steam, electricity, and atomic energy: willpower" reminds us of the innate power that resides within each of us to drive our actions and achieve our goals. Willpower is an internal and motivating force that surpasses physical limitations and allows us to persevere despite difficulties. Through practical examples, such as the story of Thomas Edison and the competitive spirit of Olympic athletes, we can understand the transformative impact of willpower in the pursuit of success and fulfillment.

"Most of the fundamental ideas of science are essentially simple, and, as a rule, can be expressed in a language comprehensible to everyone."

— Albert Einstein

SCIENCE, AT ITS core, seeks to understand the world around us through observation, logical reasoning, and experimentation. Often, the complexity and technical jargon may give the impression that scientific ideas are inaccessible to those who are not familiar with the field. However, this statement suggests that the fundamental ideas of science can be simplified and communicated in a language understandable to everyone.

A practical example of this assertion can be found in the field of astronomy and the Big Bang theory. The fundamental idea behind the Big Bang is that the universe originated from a cosmic explosion approximately 13.8 billion years ago. At first glance, this idea may seem complex and difficult to grasp, but as it is broken down and explained in simpler terms, it becomes more accessible to everyone.

Imagine we want to explain the Big Bang to a child. We could use a metaphor to make it understandable. We could say that the Big Bang was like a huge explosion of confetti in space, where all the stars, planets, and galaxies began to move away from each other. This simple analogy captures the essence of the theory and allows the child to have a basic understanding of the concept.

Furthermore, scientists and science communicators have found effective ways to communicate complex scientific ideas to the general public through outreach programs, documentaries, and popular science books. For example, theoretical physicist Stephen Hawking wrote "A Brief History of Time," a book that discusses the fundamental concepts of theoretical physics in an accessible and understandable way for the general public. Through everyday examples, analogies, and clear language, Hawking managed to convey complex scientific ideas such as relativity and black holes to a wide audience.

"**W**hoever is careless with the truth in small matters cannot be trusted with important matters.

TRUTH IS A fundamental value that should prevail in all our interactions and decisions, regardless of their magnitude. The phrase suggests that those who do not give importance to truthfulness in small matters are likely to be unreliable in more significant matters. Integrity and honesty are essential qualities that must be cultivated in all areas of our lives.

A practical example of this assertion can be found in the professional sphere. Imagine an employee who regularly exaggerates their achievements and abilities in minor tasks or projects. Although these lies may seem harmless at first, they undermine the trust and credibility of the individual. When it comes time to face more important projects, such as leading a team or managing significant financial resources, their reputation for being careless with the truth in small matters raises doubts in others about their ability to make ethical and responsible decisions.

This lack of trust can have negative consequences both personally and professionally. Coworkers and superiors may doubt their honesty, and as a result, they may miss out on opportunities for growth and development within the company. Furthermore, unreliability can affect interpersonal relationships, as people may be reluctant to collaborate or trust someone who has shown themselves to be careless with the truth in everyday situations.

On the other hand, a person who commits to being honest and truthful in all aspects of their life, even in small things, builds a reputation for integrity and trustworthiness. These qualities are especially valuable in more significant situations, such as leading a team, assuming financial responsibilities, or being a role model for others. Those who are consistent in their commitment to truthfulness inspire confidence and become respected and admired leaders.

3
Jiddu Krishnamurti

About Jiddu Krishnamurti

Jiddu Krishnamurti was an Indian philosopher and writer known for his radically different approach to life and society. Throughout his life, Krishnamurti developed a philosophy that promoted personal freedom, self-inquiry, and the transcendence of limitations imposed by society and conditioned minds.

Krishnamurti rejected any form of external authority, whether religious, political, or spiritual, and emphasized the importance of inner authority and self-knowledge. He believed that truth and wisdom could not be found through belief systems or dogmas but must be discovered through direct observation and deep inquiry into one's own mind.

For Krishnamurti, true freedom could only be achieved by transcending social and cultural conditioning, as well as the limitations imposed by one's own mind. He held that the human mind was trapped in patterns of thought and entrenched beliefs, which generated divisions and conflicts both personally and in society as a whole.

Krishnamurti advocated for the need for a radical revolution in human consciousness. He believed that only through careful observation of our thoughts, emotions, and actions could we free ourselves from the slavery of conditioned minds and experience profound transformation. This internal transformation, according to Krishnamurti, had the potential to bring about significant change in society, freeing it from violence, competition, and the relentless pursuit of power and authority.

In summary, Krishnamurti's philosophy focused on the importance of personal freedom, inner authority, and self-inquiry as means to transcend mental and social conditioning. He believed in the possibility of deep change and transformation of human consciousness, which could in turn have a positive impact on society as a whole.

Krishnamurti emphasized a wide range of topics in his philosophy. Here are some of the main themes he focused on:

1. **Self-knowledge:** Krishnamurti believed in the importance of self-discovery through direct observation of the mind and consciousness. He held that only by fully understanding our thoughts, emotions, motivations, and behavioral patterns could we free ourselves from the influence of conditioning and experience true freedom.

2. **Freedom and authority:** He rejected any form of external authority and emphasized the need to develop inner authority based on self-knowledge. He argued that only when we free ourselves from the influence of external authority and conformity to established patterns can we truly be free and act responsibly.

3. **Conditioning and conditioned mind:** Krishnamurti explored how the human mind is conditioned by society, culture, education, beliefs, and past experiences. He emphasized the need to be aware of this conditioning and question its limiting effects, seeking to free oneself from it to achieve a free and open mind.

4. **Relationships and love:** He addressed the topic of human relationships and true love. He held that our relationships are often based on dependence, fear, selfishness, and possession, and that only through selfless and unattached love can we experience authentic and meaningful relationships.

5. **Meditation and mindfulness:** Krishnamurti considered meditation not as a separate practice but as a state of mindfulness in daily life. He promoted non-judgmental observation of every thought, emotion, and action in the present, allowing for greater clarity and understanding of oneself and the world.

6. **Social transformation:** While Krishnamurti primarily focused on individual transformation, he also advocated for the possibility of significant social change. He believed that when people free themselves from their own conditioning and act with responsibility and compassion, they can contribute to the creation of a just, peaceful, and harmonious society.

These are just some of the main themes that Krishnamurti explored in his philosophy. His challenging and radical approach invites deep reflection and the search for truth beyond the limitations imposed by society and conditioned minds.

Krishnamurti had a critical view of society and formal education. He believed that society as a whole was trapped in belief systems, traditions, and hierarchical structures that generated divisions, conflicts, and suffering. He considered these social limitations as obstacles to the flourishing of true intelligence and human freedom.

Regarding formal education, Krishnamurti argued that it primarily focused on transmitting knowledge and technical skills, neglecting the holistic development of the individual. He held that the purpose of education should be to cultivate not only intellect but also sensitivity, compassion, and self-knowledge. He considered education should help students discover their own vocation and understand the importance of living a full and meaningful life.

Krishnamurti questioned the traditional approach to education that fosters competition, comparison, and conformity to established patterns. He held that this not only limits the creativity and individuality of students but also perpetuates the problems and conflicts of society.

Instead of formal education, Krishnamurti advocated for an educational approach based on freedom, self-inquiry, and attentive observation. He believed that students should be encouraged to explore and question for themselves, rather than passively accepting authority and established knowledge. He promoted an educational environment in which students and teachers could learn together, without hierarchies and without the influence of social conditioning.

In summary, Krishnamurti criticized society and formal education for their focus on conditioning, conformity, and lack of freedom and self-knowledge. He advocated for a society and education that fostered inner freedom, intelligence, and individual responsibility, thereby creating a more peaceful and harmonious world.

Wisdom Quotes by J. Krishnamurti

"Wisdom is the elimination of the known."

"Truth is a land without paths."

"Truth is what it is,
and to follow truth demands great intelligence."

"It is not a sign of good health
to be well adjusted to a deeply sick society."

"Observation without evaluation
is the highest form of human intelligence."

"The true revolution
is the revolution of consciousness."

"Happiness is not found through seeking,
but through understanding."

"Violence is the fear
of others' ideals."

"Freedom lies in being aware of our chains."

"Peace is not something achieved externally,
but born within the heart."

"Fear is not part of love,
nor is love part of fear."

"MEDITATION IS NOT A MEANS TO AN END.
IT IS THE STATE OF MIND
WHEN ALL THINGS ARE UNDERSTOOD TOGETHER."

"TRUTH IS A LAND WITHOUT PATHS
AND YOU CANNOT APPROACH IT
BY ANY PATH BY ANY RELIGION BY ANY SECT."

"Intelligence is the ability
to observe without judgment."

"FREEDOM AND REBELLION ARE NOTHING
BUT A SEARCH FOR SECURITY."

"Thought cannot lead to understanding.
Understanding arises when thought stops."

"THE TRUE REVOLUTION OCCURS SILENTLY,
INTERNALLY, AND SPREADS
WITHOUT MAKING NOISE IN SOCIETY."

"LOVE HAS NO FEAR AND SEEKS NOTHING."

My Commentary on
Jiddu Krishnamurti's Quotes

"The truth is a land without paths."

– J. Krishnamurti

TRUTH IS A complex and multifaceted concept that can be interpreted in various ways. Each individual has their own understanding and perception of what they consider to be true. In this sense, truth is a subjective experience that transcends established paths and social conventions.

The phrase suggests that truth cannot be limited by dogmas, beliefs, or pre-established structures. It cannot be reached through a single traced and predetermined path. Instead, truth requires individual exploration and a personal journey of discovery.

In our search for truth, we often encounter different paths and perspectives that may seem contradictory. Each of us has our own experiences, knowledge, and unique understandings of the world. Therefore, truth can be seen from multiple angles and cannot be contained within a single path or belief system.

A practical example of this statement can be found in the field of science and scientific theories. Throughout history, different approaches and scientific paradigms have emerged to understand the world around us. Each of these approaches has provided a particular perspective and has contributed to our accumulated knowledge. However, it is important to recognize that none of them can claim an absolute and immutable truth. Instead, science continues to evolve as new evidence is discovered and new theories are formulated.

The phrase also urges us to question our own beliefs and to keep an open mind on our journey towards truth. We are often influenced by our past experiences, teachings, and expectations. However, by freeing ourselves from predefined paths and exploring new possibilities, we can discover a broader and deeper truth.

"The truth is what it is, and to pursue the truth requires great intelligence."

– J. Krishnamurti

TRUTH REFERS TO the correspondence between our perceptions, beliefs, and objective reality. It is a fundamental concept that drives our understanding of the world and our interactions with it. However, arriving at the truth is not always an easy path and requires a constant dedication to the pursuit of knowledge and understanding.

To pursue the truth, it is necessary to cultivate an open mind and be willing to question our own ideas and pre-existing beliefs. This involves recognizing that our perceptions may be biased and that truth may be more complex and multifaceted than we initially thought. Intelligence lies in the ability to transcend our cognitive limitations and be receptive to new perspectives and evidence.

A practical example of this assertion can be found in the field of science. Scientists are dedicated to investigating and discovering the truth in different areas of knowledge. To achieve this, they must possess great intelligence to design rigorous experiments, analyze data critically, and be willing to adjust their theories based on the results. Intelligence is not only limited to having a high IQ but also to having an open, curious mind willing to challenge established assumptions in search of a more precise understanding of the truth.

Pursuing the truth also requires critical thinking and discernment. We cannot blindly accept any claim as true, but rather we must objectively evaluate it based on solid evidence. Intelligence allows us to analyze and assess the truthfulness of claims, weighing the evidence and considering different perspectives before reaching informed conclusions.

In summary, the phrase "The truth is what it is, and to pursue the truth requires great intelligence" reminds us of the importance of maintaining an open and critical mind in our search for truth. Intelligence plays a fundamental role in this process, as it allows us to question our own beliefs, objectively evaluate evidence, and be willing to adjust our viewpoints based on new information. Through practical examples such as scientific work, we can appreciate how intelligence and the pursuit of truth are closely related, as they require a keen and sharp mind to explore and understand reality more fully and accurately.

"The truth is what it is, and to pursue the truth requires great intelligence."

TRUTH REFERS TO the correspondence between our perceptions, beliefs, and objective reality. It is a fundamental concept that drives our understanding of the world and our interactions with it. However, arriving at the truth is not always an easy path and requires a constant dedication to the pursuit of knowledge and understanding.

To pursue the truth, it is necessary to cultivate an open mind and be willing to question our own ideas and pre-existing beliefs. This involves recognizing that our perceptions may be biased and that truth may be more complex and multifaceted than we initially thought. Intelligence lies in the ability to transcend our cognitive limitations and be receptive to new perspectives and evidence.

A practical example of this assertion can be found in the field of science. Scientists are dedicated to investigating and discovering the truth in different areas of knowledge. To achieve this, they must possess great intelligence to design rigorous experiments, analyze data critically, and be willing to adjust their theories based on the results. Intelligence is not only limited to having a high IQ but also to having an open, curious mind willing to challenge established assumptions in search of a more precise understanding of the truth.

Pursuing the truth also requires critical thinking and discernment. We cannot blindly accept any claim as true, but rather we must objectively evaluate it based on solid evidence. Intelligence allows us to analyze and assess the truthfulness of claims, weighing the evidence and considering different perspectives before reaching informed conclusions.

In summary, the phrase "The truth is what it is, and to pursue the truth requires great intelligence" reminds us of the importance of maintaining an open and critical mind in our search for truth. Intelligence plays a fundamental role in this process, as it allows us to question our own beliefs, objectively evaluate evidence, and be willing to adjust our viewpoints based on new information. Through practical examples such as scientific work, we can appreciate how intelligence and the pursuit of truth are closely related, as they require a keen and sharp mind to explore and understand reality more fully and accurately.

"Not being well adapted to a profoundly sick society is not a sign of good health."

– J. Krishnamurti

HEALTH IS NOT solely limited to the absence of physical illness, but encompasses emotional, mental, and social aspects as well. Being adapted to a profoundly sick society implies conforming to norms, beliefs, and behaviors that may be harmful or contrary to our deepest values.

Maintaining health involves being aware of our own integrity and well-being, even when the social environment may be in imbalance. It is an act of courage and authenticity to not succumb to social pressures and to question what we perceive as harmful or inappropriate.

True health entails being aware of external influences and making decisions that promote our physical, emotional, mental, and moral well-being. Through practical examples, such as balancing social media use or advocating for social justice, we can exercise autonomy and demonstrate greater health by not conforming to a society that goes against our deepest principles.

I believe that my health and well-being cannot be measured solely by my physical state, but also extend to my emotional, mental, and moral well-being. Reflecting on this phrase, I realize that blindly adapting to the norms and behaviors of a society I consider sick is not a sign of real health, but rather a display of complacency and conformity.

It is easy to be swept along by social currents, adopting beliefs and behaviors without questioning their validity or their impact on myself and others. However, this phrase reminds me of the importance of maintaining my integrity and staying true to my deepest values, even if it means standing out and facing the pressure of social conformity.

Being aware of injustices, inequalities, and systemic issues in society can be uncomfortable and challenging. But understanding that my health and well-being cannot be separated from the principles I stand for drives me to be an agent of change, to question the structures that perpetuate social illness, and to take actions that promote justice and equity.

At the same time, this reflection leads me to recognize that my role in transforming society is not only external but also internal. It is necessary to evaluate and question my own beliefs and actions, and be willing to course-correct if I find that I am contributing to social illness in any way.

This phrase invites me to maintain a critical and reflective attitude, to seek truth, and to act courageously based on my principles. I cannot expect society to change if I myself am not willing to change and challenge the systems and structures that perpetuate illness.

Ultimately, this reflection reminds me that my health and well-being are inexorably linked to the well-being of the society in which I live. By becoming aware of the chains and imbalances around me, I can be a positive agent of change and work to build a healthier and more equitable society, both for myself and for others.

"**F**ear is not part of love, nor is love part of fear."

– J. Krishnamurti

FEAR AND LOVE are opposite emotions and often incompatible. Fear is an emotional response that arises when we feel threatened or insecure, while love is a feeling of deep connection, acceptance, and appreciation towards ourselves and others. These two emotions have very different energies and effects in our lives.

When fear intertwines with love, imbalances and tensions occur in our relationships and in our own way of loving. Fear can manifest as jealousy, control, distrust, or emotional dependency, aspects that are not aligned with the pure essence of love. These manifestations of fear can limit our ability to love authentically and fully.

On the other hand, genuine love is characterized by trust, respect, empathy, and freedom. When we love from a place of authenticity and wholeness, there is no room for fear. True love does not seek to control or possess another person but is based on mutual support, understanding, and growth together.

An example of this assertion could be a romantic relationship where fear is present. If one member of the relationship experiences constant jealousy and distrust towards the other, this creates a toxic and limiting environment where love cannot fully blossom. Distrust and unfounded fears create barriers that hinder genuine connection and emotional intimacy.

To experience love authentically, it is necessary to address and free ourselves from our internal fears. This involves a process of self-awareness and self-transcendence, where we explore our insecurities and limiting beliefs to be able to let them go and open ourselves to a more full and liberating experience of love.

The phrase "Fear is not part of love, nor is love part of fear" reminds us of the importance of recognizing and freeing ourselves from the fears that can hinder our relationships and our ability to love authentically. True love is based on trust, acceptance, and freedom and cannot flourish in an atmosphere of fear and control. By releasing our fears, we can open ourselves to a more full and satisfying experience of love, both towards ourselves and others.

In my own life, I have experienced how fear can affect my ability to love authentically. I remember a situation where I was in a relationship where fear was a constant presence. I was afraid of being hurt, abandoned, or not being loved enough. These fears led me to behave possessively and distrustfully towards my partner.

My constant fear of losing my partner led me to question their actions, to seek evidence of their fidelity, and to try to control their behavior. I was convinced that if I could maintain strict control over the relationship, I would avoid pain and disappointment. However, this attitude only created an atmosphere of tension and restriction in our relationship.

Over time, I realized that my fear was preventing love from flourishing genuinely. I realized that love cannot thrive in a fertile ground of distrust and control. I understood that if I wanted to experience a more authentic and healthy connection, I had to confront my fears and free myself from them.

Through a process of self-exploration and self-acceptance, I began to work on my own insecurities and limiting beliefs. I recognized that fear was not part of love and that I had to stop letting it dictate my actions and emotions. I learned to trust more in myself and my ability to handle any situation that arose.

This personal example showed me that fear and love cannot coexist harmoniously. Only by freeing ourselves from our fears can we experience love in its purest and most authentic form. Freedom from fears allows us to love with openness, acceptance, and compassion, thus creating healthier and more satisfying relationships.

In conclusion, my personal experience has taught me that fear is not part of love and that it is crucial to address and free ourselves from our fears in order to love fully and authentically. By doing so, we can cultivate relationships based on trust, acceptance, and freedom, allowing love to flourish in all its splendor.

OBSERVATION REFERS TO the ability to perceive and understand the environment objectively, without issuing judgments or automatic evaluations. It implies a mindful and open attention to the details and characteristics of the object of study, whether it be a situation, a person, or a phenomenon. By observing without evaluation, we allow ourselves to see things as they are, without interference from our own mental filters.

Evaluation, on the other hand, refers to the process of judging, categorizing, and assigning value to the information we perceive. It is the result of our prejudices, beliefs, and past experiences, which influence our interpretation of the facts. Evaluation can limit our understanding and restrict our perspectives, biasing our perception of reality.

Human intelligence is manifested in our ability to observe impartially and free from judgments. By being aware of our biases and prejudices, we can avoid falling into the trap of automatic evaluation and open ourselves to a deeper and more objective understanding of things.

A practical example of this assertion could be when we find ourselves in a situation of interpersonal conflict. Instead of issuing quick judgments and reacting impulsively, we can practice observation without evaluation. This involves listening carefully to the other person, paying attention to their words, body language, and emotions, without jumping to conclusions or issuing hasty judgments.

By observing without evaluation, we open ourselves to a broader understanding of the situation and the perspectives of others. It allows us to be more empathetic and understanding, avoiding falling into the trap of prejudices and stereotypes that could cloud our vision. This form of observation helps us generate more creative and constructive solutions, promoting the resolution of conflicts in a peaceful and respectful manner.

In my own life, I have experienced how practicing observation without evaluation has allowed me to gain a greater understanding and appreciation of the diversity of ideas, opinions, and experiences that exist in the world. By freeing myself from my own prejudices, I have been able to learn from people with different perspectives and enrich my own worldview.

By being aware of our biases and prejudices, we can practice impartial observation, allowing us a clearer and more objective view of reality. This helps us make more informed decisions, promote empathy and understanding, and cultivate more harmonious and collaborative relationships."

"The true revolution is the revolution of consciousness."

– J. Krishnamurti

TRADITIONALLY, REVOLUTION IS associated with significant political, social, or technological changes in society. However, the assertion invites us to consider that the true revolution is not limited to external changes but takes place within ourselves, in the realm of our consciousness.

Consciousness refers to our ability to be aware of ourselves, our actions, thoughts, and emotions, and the interactions we have with the world around us. It is the spark that enables us to question, reflect, and seek greater knowledge and understanding.

The revolution of consciousness involves a personal awakening, a process of self-discovery, and expanding our perspective. It is about questioning entrenched ideas and beliefs we have inherited and exploring new ways of seeing and understanding the world. It is a call to transcend the limits of our conditioned mind and open ourselves to new possibilities.

A practical example of this revolution of consciousness is when we challenge ourselves to question our own preconceived ideas and explore different perspectives. Instead of clinging to our limiting beliefs, we open ourselves to new ideas, cultures, and ways of thinking. We allow ourselves to learn from others' experiences and seek a deeper understanding of life's complexities.

As we expand our consciousness, we become more aware of the injustices and challenges facing humanity. We develop greater empathy towards others and recognize our interconnectedness with all human beings and the planet itself. This motivates us to take actions that promote equality, social justice, and sustainability.

In my own life, I have experienced the revolution of consciousness as I have sought knowledge, cultivated empathy, and challenged my own mental limitations. I have learned to question my own biases and listen to the voices of those who have been marginalized or ignored. Through this expansion of consciousness, I have discovered new ways to contribute to positive change in the world.

By questioning our entrenched beliefs, opening ourselves to new ideas, and understanding our interconnectedness with others, we can take more informed and transformative actions. This revolution of consciousness propels us towards a fairer, more equitable, and sustainable world where all human beings can flourish and thrive.

"Happiness is not found through seeking, but through understanding."

– J. Krishnamurti

THE PURSUIT OF happiness is something many of us identify with. Often, we find ourselves chasing external goals, such as professional success, material possessions, or relationships, hoping they will bring us happiness and satisfaction. However, this constant pursuit can lead to a sense of perpetual dissatisfaction.

The statement invites us to consider that true happiness is not found externally, but within our internal understanding. The key lies in understanding who we truly are, what motivates us, what brings us joy and inner peace. It is a call to explore our inner world and develop greater awareness and understanding of ourselves.

Instead of seeking happiness in external things, we can find it by cultivating understanding and wisdom. This involves gaining a deeper understanding of our own emotions, thoughts, and behavior patterns. It allows us to recognize our strengths and weaknesses and accept ourselves unconditionally.

Rather than blindly following society's or others' expectations, we allow ourselves to explore what truly makes us feel fulfilled and satisfied. This may involve discovering our passions, cultivating meaningful relationships, practicing self-compassion and self-care, or seeking balance between work and personal life.

As we deepen our understanding of ourselves, we can also develop greater empathy and understanding towards others. We recognize that each individual has their own journey and internal struggles, and we learn to be more compassionate and respectful of their experiences.

I have experienced how internal understanding has been fundamental to my well-being and happiness. By taking the time to explore my own values, beliefs, and needs, I have been able to make decisions more aligned with my true self and live a more authentic life. I have also learned to appreciate and understand others' different perspectives and experiences, enriching my relationships and my ability to connect with others meaningfully.

By cultivating greater awareness of our own thoughts, emotions, and needs, and by understanding and respecting others' experiences, we can find true happiness and satisfaction in our lives. The key is to look inward and seek internal understanding as a path to lasting fulfillment and well-being.

"Violence is the fear of others' ideals."

– J. Krishnamurti

VIOLENCE IS A phenomenon that unfortunately has been present throughout human history. Often, violence arises from conflicts, differences of opinion, and a lack of understanding among people. The statement invites us to consider that violence can stem from the fear we feel towards the beliefs and ideals of others.

Fear is a powerful emotion that can drive us to act in destructive ways. When we feel threatened or insecure, we may react with violence to protect our own beliefs and perspectives. However, this fear of others' ideals can lead to an endless cycle of violence and conflict.

When we observe violent clashes between groups advocating for opposing ideologies, each group may fear that the other's ideas undermine their own values and objectives. This lack of understanding and mutual respect can lead to physical, verbal, or emotional violence, instead of fostering constructive and peaceful dialogue.

In my own life, I have experienced how fear of others' ideals can generate tension and conflict. Sometimes, when I find myself in situations where there are different viewpoints or beliefs, I may feel threatened and react defensively. However, I have learned to recognize that fear is neither constructive nor beneficial for resolving differences.

Instead of being driven by fear, I strive to cultivate empathy and understanding towards others' ideals. This involves actively listening, seeking common ground, and being willing to learn from perspectives different from my own. By understanding that we all have different ideals and beliefs, I can adopt a more peaceful and respectful approach in my interactions with others.

When we cling to our own perspectives and fear that others' ideas threaten us, we are more likely to respond with violence. However, by cultivating empathy, understanding, and respect towards others, we can break this cycle of violence and work towards peaceful and constructive solutions. The key lies in overcoming our fears and embracing the diversity of ideals as an opportunity for growth and peaceful coexistence.

"The peace is not something achieved externally, but born within the heart."

– J. Krishnamurti

THE PHRASE "THE peace is not something achieved externally, but born within the heart" has deeply resonated with me and has led me to reflect on the true origin of peace. In first person, I can share my interpretation of this statement and how I have experienced it in my own life.

For a long time, I believed that peace was something found outside of myself, in external circumstances. I thought that if I could achieve financial stability, harmonious relationships, or a tranquil environment, I would find the peace I longed for. However, over time, I realized that this external pursuit of peace was ineffective and fleeting.

The statement invites us to look inward and recognize that authentic peace does not depend on external factors, but arises from internal serenity and harmony. True peace is a state of inner well-being that originates in the heart, in our attitude, and in how we choose to face life's situations.

In my own life, I have experienced how cultivating peace in my heart has transformed my way of being and relating to the world around me. When I learned to nurture my inner peace through the practice of mindfulness, meditation, and self-reflection, I discovered that I could maintain calm and serenity even in the midst of challenges and adversities.

An example of this idea is when I find myself in stressful or conflictive situations. Instead of being swept away by anxiety or anger, I strive to connect with my inner peace. I take a moment to breathe deeply, to remember my values, and to address the situation from a place of compassion and understanding.

I have learned that my own tranquility can influence the environment around me, generating a positive effect on the people I interact with. The peace in my heart becomes a gift that I can share with the world.

Authentic peace is not found in external circumstances, but born within the heart and cultivated through mindfulness and self-reflection. By nurturing our inner peace, we can face life's challenges with calmness and compassion, and contribute to a more peaceful and harmonious environment. The key is to recognize that peace is an internal journey and to commit to the daily practice of cultivating it in our hearts."

"Wisdom is the elimination of the known."

– J. Krishnamurti

MANY TIMES, WISDOM is often associated with the accumulation of knowledge and experiences. However, this phrase invites us to consider that true wisdom does not reside solely in the mere acquisition of information, but in the ability to transcend the limitations imposed by preconceived ideas and open oneself to new possibilities.

Wisdom manifests when individuals are willing to question and free themselves from entrenched beliefs and established concepts. It requires an open and flexible approach that allows for the exploration of the unknown and the discovery of a deeper understanding of reality.

When people are faced with situations where their beliefs and perspectives conflict with those of others, wisdom lies in being willing to listen and understand different viewpoints, even if they differ from one's own. This involves overcoming mental rigidity and adopting an attitude of openness towards new ideas and perspectives.

The elimination of the known also implies recognizing the limits of our own knowledge and being willing to learn from others. It is acknowledging that we do not know everything and that there is always room for growth and expansion of understanding. Wisdom is nourished by intellectual humility and the willingness to recognize that there is always more to discover.

Wisdom is not just about accumulating knowledge, but about having the willingness and mental openness to question and move beyond preconceived ideas. It is the ability to explore the unknown and embrace new perspectives. Wisdom is found in those who are willing to learn from others and recognize the limits of their own knowledge. It is a path towards a deeper and more meaningful understanding of reality.

For much of my life, I associated wisdom with accumulating knowledge and facts. I believed that the more I knew about the world and its complexities, the wiser I would be. However, over time, I realized that true wisdom does not reside in the accumulation of information, but in the ability to set aside our preconceived ideas and open ourselves to new perspectives.

The assertion invites us to question and free ourselves from the limitations imposed by our entrenched beliefs and preconceived ideas. Wisdom lies in being willing to let go of our assumptions and open ourselves to the unknown. By letting go of what we already "know," we open ourselves to new possibilities and a deeper understanding of reality.

I have found that wisdom is revealed when I am willing to question my own beliefs and challenge what I consider to be absolute truths. When I free myself from mental rigidity and open myself to different viewpoints, I can expand my understanding and approach wisdom.

In situations where my opinions or perspectives clash with those of others, instead of stubbornly clinging to my own ideas, I try to listen and understand the viewpoints of others. This involves setting aside ego and being open to learning something new, even if it means challenging or letting go of my previous beliefs.

The elimination of the known also relates to intellectual humility and the willingness to acknowledge that we do not know everything. As I learn more and more, I realize that there is a vast ocean of knowledge that is still beyond my reach. Wisdom lies in accepting this humility and continuing to seek, always willing to learn and grow.

"Meditation is not a means to an end. It is the state of mind when all things are understood together."

– J. Krishnamurti

AT TIMES, MEDITATION is often seen as a means to achieve a specific goal, such as relaxation, stress reduction, or personal development. However, this phrase invites us to consider that meditation goes beyond being a simple means to attain a desired end.

Meditation is a state of mind in which a deep understanding of all things together is experienced. It is a state of clarity and connection that transcends the barriers of conditioned mind and allows us to see the interconnections between phenomena and understand the nature of reality.

When people engage in regular meditation practice, they may experience a state of being in which the mind quiets and expands, allowing for greater perception and understanding of the entirety of existence. In this state, the limitations of dualistic and fragmented mind dissolve, and a sense of unity and connection with everything around us can be experienced.

As people sit down to meditate and direct their attention inward, they may experience moments of profound clarity and understanding where ideas and concepts come together and become transparent. It's as if all the pieces of a puzzle fit together, and the complete picture can be perceived.

Meditation is not just about focusing on a specific goal or outcome, but about allowing the mind to open and expand to grasp the totality of the present experience. In this state of mindfulness, the deeper and subtler connections between all things can be understood, and a sense of integration and unity can be experienced.

Meditation is a state of mind in which all things are understood together. By practicing meditation regularly, people can experience greater understanding and connection with the entirety of existence. Meditation invites us to transcend the limitations of conditioned mind and open ourselves to a deeper and more meaningful experience of reality.

I used to think of meditation as a tool to achieve certain goals, such as calmness, emotional balance, or mental clarity. However, over time, I realized that meditation goes beyond that. It is a state of mind in which a deep understanding of reality and a connection with all things occurs.

When I meditate, I don't seek to achieve a specific outcome. I don't try to force calmness or eliminate thoughts. Instead, I immerse myself in the present moment and allow my mind to calm and settle. It is in this state of mental stillness where I can experience greater clarity and understanding of the interconnection of all things.

During meditation, I can observe how my thoughts, emotions, and sensations arise and dissolve in my awareness. As I practice mindfulness, I can see how all these phenomena are interconnected and how they affect my overall experience. It's like looking at a puzzle where all the pieces come together to form a complete picture.

Meditation has taught me that it's not about achieving an ideal mental state or attaining certain external results. It's about being present and understanding the nature of reality as it presents itself in each moment. It is in this state of mindful awareness where I can experience greater peace, clarity, and connection with everything around me.

Meditation invites me to be present and cultivate a mindful awareness that transcends superficial goals and connects me with the essence of reality.

"Truth is a land without paths, and you cannot approach it by any path, by any religion, by any sect."

– J. Krishnamurti

FROM MY PERSONAL experience, I have come to understand that truth is something that goes beyond the labels and divisions imposed by religions or sects. It is not found in adherence to a single doctrine but in the ability to question, investigate, and discover for oneself.

The pursuit of truth involves a process of self-inquiry and personal discernment. It requires an open mind willing to question preconceived ideas and deeply rooted belief systems. Instead of following a path laid out by others, it is necessary to explore our own experience and understand our own internal truths.

Each person may have their own understanding of truth, and it is in respect and openness to diverse interpretations that we can approach a broader and more enriching view of reality.

Truth cannot be confined by predefined paths, religions, or sects. It is a land without paths that requires personal exploration and an open mind. Each individual has the capacity to discover their own truth through introspection and questioning. The pursuit of truth involves openness to different perspectives and the understanding that truth can be subjective and multidimensional.

In the pursuit of truth, some people may feel the need to follow a path established by a particular religion or sect. However, this phrase suggests that truth cannot be confined to a single path or belief system. No matter how elaborate or ancient a path may be, truth transcends its confines.

The phrase also suggests that truth is one's own path, not dictated by others but discovered through self-inquiry and personal discernment. Each individual has their own journey in the pursuit of truth and may find it in unique experiences and personal connections with the world around them.

Truth transcends established beliefs and is found in personal exploration and openness to different perspectives. Each individual has the capacity to discover their own truth through self-inquiry and personal discernment.

"Intelligence is the ability to observe without judging."

– J. Krishnamurti

INTELLIGENCE IS DEMONSTRATED when a person has the capacity to observe with attention and understanding, without being swayed by hasty judgments or preconceived biases. Those who possess this quality are capable of examining facts and situations objectively, without allowing emotions or personal opinions to influence their perception.

In society, it is common to encounter individuals who, instead of observing without judging, tend to form quick opinions and make value judgments about others or situations. These judgments may be based on preconceptions, stereotypes, or deeply held beliefs. However, those with true intelligence understand the importance of suspending judgment and seeing beyond appearances.

The ability to observe without judging can also be applied to social interactions. A person who is capable of listening attentively without prejudice, without labeling or categorizing others, demonstrates a form of emotional and social intelligence. This allows them to understand others on a deeper level and establish relationships based on respect and mutual understanding.

Those who possess this quality are capable of examining facts and situations objectively, without allowing judgments and prejudices to influence their perception. This impartial observation can have a positive impact on work environments, social interactions, and informed decision-making.

In my personal journey, I have encountered situations where the temptation to judge quickly and superficially arises naturally. However, I have learned that it is necessary to pause and take a more objective and impartial approach. By doing so, I can appreciate the richness and complexity of people and situations without being swayed by assumptions or stereotypes.

A practical example of how I apply this ability to observe without judging in my life is when I interact with people who have opinions or perspectives different from mine. Instead of jumping to hasty conclusions or closing myself off to my own point of view, I strive to listen attentively and understand their motivations, experiences, and values. By doing so, I can engage in constructive and respectful dialogue, and enrich my own understanding of the world.

Likewise, this ability to observe without judging also applies to my relationship with myself. Often, we judge ourselves harshly and impose impossible standards to meet. However, I have learned to adopt a more compassionate and understanding stance towards my own actions and decisions. Instead of constantly criticizing myself, I seek to understand my motivations, learn from my mistakes, and cultivate a sense of self-acceptance and self-love.

Through my personal experience, I have learned that intelligence involves the ability to observe without judging. Instead of allowing prejudices and subjective evaluations to influence my perception, I strive to maintain an open and understanding mind. This allows me to appreciate the diversity of perspectives, establish deeper connections with others, and cultivate a more positive relationship with myself. The ability to observe without judging is a path towards understanding, respect, and personal growth."

"Love has no fear and seeks nothing."

– J. Krishnamurti

THOSE WHO LOVE authentically are not afraid to open their hearts and be vulnerable. They do not cling to expectations or selfish desires but offer their love without expecting anything in return. This unconditional love is selfless and does not seek to satisfy its own needs or gains.

In society, we often find relationships based on fear and desire. Some people fear losing their loved ones, so they try to control or manipulate the other person. Others seek to fill an emotional void through love and seek personal gratification. However, those who truly understand the essence of love understand that it transcends fear and does not seek personal satisfaction.

When two people love and genuinely care for each other, they are not threatened by each other's success or happiness. They do not fear losing the other person but instead support and encourage them in their personal growth and development. Their love is selfless and based on deep respect and mutual acceptance.

Moreover, love that seeks nothing also manifests in altruistic actions and service to others. Those who love genuinely find satisfaction in providing support, compassion, and care to those around them without expecting recognition or reward. Their love is expressed through acts of kindness and generosity, without seeking personal benefits.

Authentic love is not based on fear and does not seek to satisfy selfish desires. Those who truly love are not afraid to be vulnerable and offer their love without expecting anything in return. This form of unconditional love is reflected in strong relationships and altruistic actions. Love that has no fear and seeks nothing is selfless and compassionate love that transcends the limitations of the ego and builds deep and meaningful connections.

"

When I love without fear, I allow myself to be vulnerable and authentic in my relationships. I am not afraid to show myself as I am and open my heart to others. This courage allows me to experience a deep and meaningful connection with the people I love. I do not feel the need to protect myself or hide my emotions but trust that genuine love will be received and reciprocated.

Moreover, when I love without seeking anything in return, I can free myself from attachment and expectations. I do not seek to satisfy my own needs or selfish desires through love. Instead, my focus is on the well-being and happiness of the loved one. My love becomes an act of generosity and selfless giving, where the main goal is the flourishing and joy of the other.

Instead of expecting something in return, I am simply present and available to listen and offer my unconditional support. My love is expressed through my ability to provide comfort and encouragement without expecting rewards or personal gratification.

Furthermore, love that seeks nothing is also reflected in acts of kindness towards others and selfless service. When I engage in activities or projects that benefit others without expecting recognition or retribution, I am demonstrating a love that transcends the ego and focuses on collective well-being.

Loving with fear is not possible. Love that has no fear and seeks nothing is authentic and transcendent love that can transform our relationships and our way of relating to the world.

"**F**reedom and rebellion
are nothing but a search for security."

– J. Krishnamurti

OFTEN, THOSE WHO crave freedom seek to escape situations or circumstances they perceive as oppressive or restrictive. They may rebel against systems, norms, or structures they view as limiting in order to find a sense of security and well-being in their lives. Their quest for freedom is driven by the desire to find a space where they feel protected and free from threats or constraints.

A practical example of this dynamic can be observed in social and political movements. Many times, people come together in protests and demonstrations to fight for their freedom and rights. Rebellion arises as a response to situations they consider unjust or that prevent them from living according to their values and basic needs. In their quest for security, they seek to change the status quo and create an environment where they feel protected and can exercise their freedom.

It is important to note that this search for security through freedom and rebellion can lead to different outcomes. Some individuals may find the desired security by achieving significant changes in their environment, while others may discover that true security is not necessarily found in external freedom, but in cultivating internal security based on acceptance and authenticity.

The pursuit of freedom and rebellion are often motivated by the desire to find security and protection. People struggle to free themselves from oppressive situations and restrictions to find a sense of security in their lives. However, it is important to recognize that true security may not be exclusively linked to external freedom, but also to building internal security based on acceptance and authenticity.

I have felt the need to rebel against the restrictions and limitations I perceived in my environment. In those moments, my quest for freedom was driven by the desire to find security and protection. I felt that breaking free from the chains of established norms and expectations would allow me to live in a more authentic way aligned with my needs and desires.

A practical example of this connection can be found in my work experience. If I have ever felt trapped in a job that did not satisfy me or that limited me, my desire to find freedom and fulfillment has driven me to rebel against that situation. I have sought new opportunities or even embarked on my own professional path with the goal of finding security and satisfaction in my career.

However, as I have reflected more deeply on this relationship between freedom, rebellion, and security, I have come to understand that true security is not always found in the external pursuit of freedom. Genuine security lies in cultivating internal connection and a sense of well-being that does not depend solely on external circumstances.

Instead of seeking security through external freedom or rebellion against established norms, I have learned to find security in cultivating my own inner peace, accepting circumstances I cannot change, and trusting in my own abilities and internal resources. This internal security provides me with a sense of calm and confidence, even in challenging or restrictive situations.

True security is not exclusively found in external freedom, but in the cultivation of internal security based on acceptance and trust. By balancing the pursuit of freedom with the construction of enduring internal security, I can find a greater sense of peace and fulfillment in my life.

"Thought cannot lead to understanding. Understanding arises when thought stops."

– J. Krishnamurti

FROM THIS PERSPECTIVE, it is observed that thought is a mental activity involving processing information, analyzing, interpreting, and forming ideas and concepts.

Understanding, on the other hand, goes beyond mere thought and refers to a deeper and more direct apprehension of reality. Understanding arises when thought stops, when the mind quiets down and becomes receptive, allowing for a clearer and unfiltered perception of reality as it is.

When we encounter something new, our thought springs into action trying to comprehend and assimilate the information. However, if we cling solely to our preconceived ideas or memory, which are deeply rooted beliefs or habitual ways of thinking, our understanding may be limited. But if we are able to temporarily suspend that conditioned thought and open ourselves to the possibility of new perspectives, we can access a deeper and more authentic understanding.

The difference between intelligence and thought is that intelligence goes beyond thought and memory. Intelligence refers to the ability to perceive, understand, adapt, and solve problems creatively. While thought may be limited by our past experiences or acquired information, intelligence can open us to innovative approaches.

Intelligence, in turn, transcends memory-based thought and allows us to explore new perspectives and creative solutions. By understanding this difference and cultivating an open mind and flexible intelligence, we can expand our understanding and have a deeper insight into reality.

From my personal experience, I have observed that thought is a mental activity I constantly use to process information, analyze situations, and form ideas and opinions. Thought is an important tool for understanding the world around me and making informed decisions. However, I have noticed that mere thinking does not necessarily guarantee the presence of intelligence.

Intelligence goes beyond mere thought. It involves the ability to perceive, understand, and apply knowledge effectively. Intelligence implies mental flexibility, adaptability, and the ability to solve problems creatively. Through intelligence, I can see beyond my own preconceived ideas and consider different perspectives and approaches. Intelligence allows me to learn from my experiences, assimilate new information, and apply it meaningfully in various situations.

However, I have noticed that thought can be limited by my own memory, entrenched beliefs, and conditioned thought patterns. At times, I may find myself trapped in rigid and repetitive thinking, unable to consider new ideas or creative solutions. In those moments, I can recognize that my thinking does not necessarily reflect an open and flexible intelligence.

When faced with a new topic or challenge, my initial thinking may be influenced by what I already know and my pre-existing beliefs. However, as I delve into the topic and open myself to different perspectives, I can broaden my understanding and apply my intelligence to connect ideas, solve problems, and generate new insights.

In summary, from my first-person perspective, I have observed that intelligence goes beyond thought and encompasses the ability to perceive, understand, and apply knowledge effectively. While thought is a valuable tool, recognizing that intelligence includes an open mindset, flexibility, and creativity has allowed me to develop a deeper understanding of the world and make smarter decisions in my life.

"The true revolution occurs silently, internally, and spreads without making noise in society."

– J. Krishnamurti

IT IS SAID that the true revolution is one that does not seek to attract attention or create external commotion, but rather gestates within each individual. It is a profound and meaningful change in the way of thinking, acting, and relating to the world around us. This internal revolution is based on the transformation of one's own consciousness and the awakening of greater understanding and awareness.

Unlike external revolutions, which are often characterized by massive movements, noisy protests, and visible political changes, the true revolution occurs in the silence of reflection and introspection. It is an individual process in which each person questions their own beliefs, values, and behavioral patterns. It involves freeing oneself from the limitations imposed by society, conditioning, and external expectations.

This type of silent revolution is not imposed through force or violence, but rather spreads subtly and gradually. As each individual undergoes internal transformation, their influence expands to those around them. Personal change becomes a seed planted in society, generating a silent yet powerful contagion effect.

It is an individual process of reflection and consciousness change that, as it expands, has a lasting impact on how we relate to the world. It is an internal process in which I question my entrenched beliefs, examine my actions, and seek greater authenticity in my thoughts and behaviors.

As I embrace this internal revolution, my way of relating to the world begins to change. It is not a noisy or aggressive change, but rather a quiet and gradual transformation that spreads through my actions and the way I relate to others.

The true revolution does not seek to forcibly change the external world, but rather to transform my own way of seeing and experiencing the world. Through introspection and connection with my own truth, I can positively influence my environment without the need to make noise or impose my ideas.

It is through my own conscious evolution that I can have a significant impact on society. Authenticity and the pursuit of truth become the foundations of this personal revolution, which spreads without making noise, but with a transformative power in my life and in the lives of those around me."

Jorge Luis Borges

About Jorge Luis Borges

Jorge Luis Borges, the renowned Argentine writer, was characterized by his deep skepticism and fascination with concepts of reality, time, knowledge, and identity. Borges was known for his agnostic stance and his relativistic view of truth.

Regarding life and society, Borges adopted a contemplative and reflective attitude. He developed a philosophical perspective that questioned absolute certainties and explored the nature of human experience. His literature, often characterized by elements of fiction and fantasy, reflected his interest in the labyrinths of the mind and the pursuit of knowledge.

Borges was also deeply interested in time and memory, exploring the idea of how our perceptions and memories shape our reality. In his work, he often challenged traditional notions of history and identity, arguing that they are subjective and ever-changing constructions.

Overall, Borges' philosophy focused on exploring the nature of reality and understanding the human condition. His approach was more metaphysical and literary than political or social, and his writing challenged traditional structures and preconceived ideas to invite reflection and self-examination.

Jorge Luis Borges had a particular view on formal education and individual creativity. While it is important to note that his opinions may vary at different times in his life and work, certain recurring aspects can be identified.

Borges was not an enthusiastic advocate of formal education in the conventional sense. He considered that the traditional educational system, based on memorization and repetition of knowledge, limited critical thinking and creativity. He himself had experienced frustrations in his schooling experience and believed that true education should foster free thinking, imagination, and exploration of ideas.

Regarding individual creativity, Borges valued the ability to imagine and create new realities. He considered literature and writing as forms of expression of human creativity and advocated for the importance of imagination in life and literary work. He believed that creativity was a manifestation of individual freedom and that each person had the ability to explore and develop their own vision of the world.

Borges also emphasized the importance of reading as a source of inspiration and as a means to broaden the individual's horizon. He valued the ability of books to transport readers to different places and times and considered reading essential for intellectual development and open-mindedness.

In summary, Borges saw formal education as limiting in stimulating the creativity and imagination of the individual. He valued freedom of thought and the ability to create new realities as fundamental expressions of humanity.

Wisdom Quotes by Jorge Luis Borges

"CARE MUST BE TAKEN WHEN CHOOSING ENEMIES BECAUSE ONE ENDS UP RESEMBLING THEM."

"Let each man build his own cathedral. Why live off others' old works of art?"

"UNIVERSAL HISTORY IS THAT OF A SINGLE"

THERE MAY BE ENEMIES OF MY OPINIONS, BUT I MYSELF, IF I WAIT A WHILE, CAN ALSO BE AN ENEMY OF MY OPINIONS."

"ONE IS NOT WHAT ONE IS BECAUSE OF WHAT ONE WRITES BUT BECAUSE OF WHAT ONE HAS READ."

"WE ALL WALK TOWARDS ANONYMITY, ONLY THE MEDIOCRE ARRIVE A LITTLE EARLIER."

"LITERATURE IS NOTHING BUT A DIRECTED DREAM."

"ONLY THAT WHICH HAS GONE IS WHAT BELONGS TO US."

"Happiness does not need to be transmuted into beauty, but misfortune does."

"I HAVE SOMETIMES SUSPECTED THAT THE ONLY THING WITHOUT MYSTERY IS HAPPINESS, BECAUSE IT JUSTIFIES ITSELF."

"OVER THE YEARS I HAVE OBSERVED
THAT BEAUTY, LIKE HAPPINESS, IS FREQUENT.
NOT A DAY GOES BY WHEN WE ARE NOT,
FOR A MOMENT, IN PARADISE."

"I do not speak of vengeance or forgiveness,
forgetfulness is the only vengeance
and the only forgiveness."

"TYRANNIES FOSTER STUPIDITY."

"DO NOT SPEAK UNLESS
YOU CAN IMPROVE ON SILENCE."

"IN MY NEXT LIFE
I WILL TRY TO MAKE MORE MIS
TAKES."

"FROM MY WEAKNESS,
I OBTAINED A STRENGTH
THAT NEVER ABANDONED ME."

"Poets, like the blind,
can see in the darkness."

"TRUTH NEVER PENETRATES
A MIND UNWILLING TO RECEIVE IT."

My Commentary on
Jorge Luis Borges
Quotes

"It is necessary to be careful when choosing enemies because one ends up resembling them."

– Jorge Luis Borges

WHEN I CONSIDER myself an enemy of someone, I enter a state of tension and resistance. My mind focuses on rivalry and proving my superiority over the other person. However, in doing so, I find myself trapped in a cycle of negativity and animosity that not only affects my relationship with that person but also my emotional well-being.

Constant rivalry and enmity not only influence my external relationships but also have an internal impact. My thoughts become obsessive, my energy is consumed in fueling the conflict, and my inner peace is disturbed. I find myself trapped in a dynamic that takes me away from the serenity and harmony I desire.

Once I dive into limitless confrontation, I lose sight of what really matters. I focus on competition and proving my superiority, instead of cultivating empathy, understanding, and human connection. Instead of finding a peaceful and constructive solution, I am drawn into an endless cycle of confrontation and resentment.

The paradox is that by considering having enemies, I end up limiting myself. My vision narrows, and my capacity for growth and learning is hindered. Instead of cultivating compassion and wisdom, I am entrenched in the defensive stance of remaining an enemy to someone.

It is important to remember that life is not about winning battles against imaginary enemies. It is about finding inner peace, connection, and personal growth. By freeing myself from the mentality of having enemies, I can make room for mutual understanding, cooperation, and building healthy relationships.

When someone considers themselves an enemy of another person, a dynamic of confrontation and competition is established. Thoughts and actions focus on demonstrating superiority and harming the other, creating an atmosphere of hostility and negativity. However, this focus on rivalry ultimately affects both parties, imprisoning them in a cycle of conflict with no clear solution.

Rivalry and enmity not only affect the relationship between people but also their emotional well-being. Obsessive thoughts, anger, and resentment take center stage in their minds, preventing effective communication and mutual understanding. This constant confrontation not only damages the relationship but also affects the internal state of individuals, causing stress, anxiety, and frustration.

The paradox lies in the fact that, by considering having enemies, people limit themselves. The possibility of cultivating compassion, empathy, and seeking peaceful solutions is lost sight of. Instead of focusing on personal growth and building healthy relationships, they become embroiled in constant battle, missing the opportunity to learn and grow as individuals.

"Let every man build his own cathedral. Why live off others' old and foreign works of art?"

– Jorge Luis Borges

IN THEIR ESSENCE, human beings are creative souls, with the innate ability to shape their reality. Like architects of a personal universe, they transcend the limitations imposed by time and space, rising above preexisting structures. Each carries within themselves the potential to build a unique legacy, a testament to their passion and purpose.

The cathedrals they build are not of stone or marble, but of dreams woven with the thread of their imagination. With each bold thought, each vision rooted in the depths of their being, they raise towers of infinite possibilities. Their hands become brushes and their words melodies, tracing majestic arches and celestial vaults in the intangible space of the spirit.

By rejecting living in the shadow of others' old and foreign masterpieces, they surrender to the dance of inspiration and originality. They venture on a journey of inner discovery, where each stone laid and each detail carved brings them closer to the fullness of their being. In every creative effort, they find a unique and genuine form of expression, leaving an indelible mark on the tapestry of life.

In the workshop of existence, the canvas unfolds like a sea of infinite possibilities. With mastery and courage, beings immerse themselves in the creative current, experimenting with colors and shapes until their souls vibrate in harmony with the work in progress. Thus, enigmatic cathedrals emerge, where each stroke reveals a fragment of their deepest essence.

In the universe of personal cathedrals, diversity is the dominant note. Each construction stands as a unique testimony to individuality and authenticity. Through their creations, human beings transcend time and leave a lasting legacy, inspiring and guiding future generations on their own journey of self-discovery.

So let every man and woman rise as architects of their own destiny, building ethereal cathedrals where their dreams find a home. In each brushstroke, in each note, in each word, they leave an imprint on the canvas of existence, woven with love, passion, and an unbreakable desire to live life in its purest expression.

In my essence, I am a creative soul, with the innate ability to shape my reality. As the architect of my own universe, I transcend the limitations imposed by time and space, rising above preexisting structures. I carry within me the potential to build a singular legacy, a testament to my passion and purpose.

The cathedral I build is not of stone or marble, but of dreams woven with the thread of my imagination. With each bold thought, each vision rooted in the depths of my being, I raise towers of infinite possibilities. My hands become brushes and my words melodies, tracing majestic arches and celestial vaults in the intangible space of my spirit.

I reject living in the shadow of others' old and foreign masterpieces. I surrender to the dance of inspiration and originality. I venture on a journey of inner discovery, where each stone laid and each detail carved brings me closer to the fullness of my being. In every creative effort, I find a unique and genuine form of expression, leaving an indelible mark on the tapestry of life.

In the workshop of my existence, the canvas unfolds like a sea of infinite possibilities. With mastery and courage, I immerse myself in the creative current, experimenting with colors and shapes until my soul vibrates in harmony with the work in progress. Thus, enigmatic cathedrals emerge, where each stroke reveals a fragment of my deepest essence.

In my universe of personal cathedrals, diversity is the dominant note. My construction stands as a unique testimony to my individuality and authenticity. Through my creations, I transcend time and leave a lasting legacy, inspiring and guiding future generations on their own journey of self-discovery.

So I rise as the architect of my own destiny, building an ethereal cathedral where my dreams find a home. In each brushstroke, in each note, in each word, I leave an imprint on the canvas of my existence, woven with love, passion, and an unbreakable desire to live life in its purest expression.

"The Universal History is that of a single man."

– Jorge Luis Borges

UNIVERSAL HISTORY UNFOLDS like a complex and diverse mosaic, whose guiding thread is humanity as a whole. Through the sum of individual and collective experiences, the plot of a single man is revealed, a collective entity that transcends divisions and borders, in search of a deeper understanding of our common past, present, and future.

From an objective perspective, this statement can be understood as the idea that the patterns and cognitive, emotional, and perceptual processes that characterize a person are fundamental and are repeated to a greater or lesser extent throughout humanity.

If we consider the ability to think, feel, and perceive as key elements of the human mind, we can identify certain common aspects in our experience. For example, the fact that all human beings have the ability to experience basic emotions such as love, joy, fear, or sadness, regardless of their culture or social context.

A practical example of this statement lies in the ability to empathize. Although individual experiences vary, all human beings possess the ability to understand and share the emotions of others. When witnessing someone else's suffering, we can feel compassion and empathy, leading us to act to alleviate their pain. This ability to empathize with others is a universal aspect of the human mind and underscores the connection and similarity we share as a species.

Another practical example can be the ability for logical reasoning and learning. Although individuals may have different levels of skill and knowledge in specific areas, we all possess an inherent capacity to reason, analyze information, and acquire new knowledge. This capacity for learning and logical reasoning is shared by all human beings and is an essential part of our collective mind.

Although people differ in many aspects, as individuals we share cognitive, emotional, and perceptual patterns that unite us as a species. This understanding invites us to value our similarity and recognize the importance of empathy, logical reasoning, and other shared qualities in building a more compassionate and supportive society.

Beyond superficial socio-cultural differences, I can affirm that the mind of one man is to some extent that of all men. Throughout my life, I have observed that there are universal aspects in our way of thinking, feeling, and perceiving the world, which transcend our individual differences.

While it is true that each individual has a unique perspective and different personal experiences, it is also evident that there are fundamental elements of the human mind that are universal. Understanding this has led me to recognize the importance of empathy and respect towards others, as we share a common ground in our way of thinking and feeling.

Recognizing this connection invites us to develop greater empathy and understanding towards others, and to work together to build a more inclusive and compassionate society.

IT IS COMMON that, at a certain moment, we firmly hold an opinion or belief. However, as we continue to grow and learn, it's possible to find ourselves in disagreement with our previous opinions. Our thought axis can shift due to new information, deeper reflections, or a change in our life circumstances.

A practical example of this could be our view on a political issue. At one point, we might have a deeply rooted opinion based on our experiences and limited knowledge. However, as we expose ourselves to different perspectives, become more informed about the topic, and reflect on its implications, our opinion might drastically change.

It's important to recognize that this ability to change our opinions and be critical of ourselves is a sign of growth and open-mindedness. Through self-assessment and continuous reflection, we can recognize our own limitations and challenge our entrenched beliefs. This doesn't imply that our opinions are necessarily incorrect or that we should constantly flip-flop, but rather that we are willing to question our own ideas and consider new perspectives.

The phrase also highlights the importance of self-criticism and the ability to be aware of our own biases and prejudices. Acknowledging that even we ourselves can become enemies of our own opinions urges us to examine our beliefs with greater objectivity and humility. By doing so, we can enrich our understanding of the world and be more open to constructive dialogue with those who hold different opinions.

It's crucial to understand that the process of changing our opinions and being critical of ourselves doesn't necessarily imply contradiction or inconsistency. Instead, it reflects the perpetual theoretical nature of our minds and our capacity for intellectual growth.

Our minds are dynamic and adaptable organs constantly seeking to expand their understanding and knowledge. As we acquire new experiences, encounter different perspectives, and engage in continuous learning, our worldview may shift and evolve. This doesn't mean that our previous opinions were wrong, but rather that we are in a constant process of reassessment and adjustment.

Understanding the perpetual theoretical nature of our minds entails accepting that our current opinions may be revisited and amended in the future. It's not about abandoning our convictions or denying the importance of taking a stance, but rather recognizing that we are always evolving. This attitude allows us to be more receptive to new ideas and perspectives, enriching our thinking and providing us with a deeper understanding of the world.

By embracing the perpetual theoretical nature of our minds, we also develop a more open and tolerant mindset towards the opinions of others. We recognize that we are all on a journey of growth and that our ideas may be complemented or challenged by those of others. This fosters constructive dialogue and enables us to draw from the diversity of thought.

By understanding that our opinions are flexible and subject to evolution, we open ourselves to greater intellectual growth and deeper understanding of the world. This approach invites us to cultivate an attitude of openness, curiosity, and humility in our interactions with others and in our own thought process.

"One is not what one is
because of what one writes,
but because of what one has read."

– Jorge Luis Borges

BORGES WAS KNOWN for his passion for books and his vast knowledge of universal literature.

In relation to the phrase "One is not what one is because of what one writes, but because of what one has read," Borges could reflect on the importance of reading as a fundamental source of inspiration and personal formation. For him, reading was a way to connect with the ideas and thoughts of other writers, as well as to explore different worlds and perspectives.

Borges could emphasize that through reading, we broaden our horizons and acquire knowledge and understanding of the world. By immersing ourselves in literature, we access a wealth of ideas, experiences, and emotions that enrich us and shape our worldview.

Our own writings reflect the amalgam of literary influences we have absorbed throughout our lives. Each book we read provides us with a new perspective, expands our vocabulary, and enriches our repertoire of images and metaphors. These influences manifest consciously or unconsciously in our writing.

Furthermore, Borges could highlight that reading allows us to delve into the minds of other writers and understand their worldview. Through reading, we connect with humanity and immerse ourselves in the ideas and emotions shared by people from different times and places.

However, Jorge Luis Borges deeply explored the theme of memory and its influence on our perception of the world. While it is true that Borges considered memory to play a fundamental role in constructing our identity and understanding reality, his view was not limited solely to the idea that we are only memory.

Borges explored the complexity of memory and its relationship with time, fiction, and perception. In many of his stories and essays, he reflected on how memory shapes our existence and how memories influence how we understand the past and construct our vision of the present.

However, Borges also addressed other dimensions of human existence, such as imagination, literature, and interpretation. He considered reality to be subjective and that our perception of the world is influenced both by our memories and by our experiences and creative thinking.

For Borges, memory was an essential component in our relationship with the past and in constructing our identity, but he also valued the ability of imagination and interpretation to shape our understanding of reality. He recognized that we are complex beings and that our existence transcends largely the dimension of memory.

In conclusion, Borges saw memory as an important element in shaping our experience and knowledge, but he did not limit our existence solely to it. His vision encompassed multiple dimensions of human life, including creativity, interpretation, and the ability to imagine and transcend the limits of memory.

"We all walk towards anonymity, it's just that the mediocre arrive a little earlier."

– Jorge Luis Borges

WE WALK TOWARDS anonymity, that is, towards physical death and the eventual disappearance of our name and form. However, those who settle for mediocrity reach that anonymity earlier, as they have relinquished their creative power and have ceased to seek deep meaning in their lives.

Each individual has the potential to live an extraordinary and meaningful life. However, most people choose to settle for a mediocre existence, allowing their fears, conditioning, and concerns to prevent them from realizing their full potential.

Self-awareness and authenticity allow us to discover and question our limiting beliefs and to live according to our own inner truth, rather than blindly following the norms and expectations imposed by society.

The phrase suggests that the ultimate fate of all human beings is anonymity, that is, eventual disappearance and oblivion. This implies that no matter how outstanding or successful we are in life, sooner or later we will reach a point where our existence fades into collective memory.

In this context, "mediocre" refers to those who settle for a common life, without standing out or reaching a level of excellence or transcendence in their actions. It is important to note that this reference to mediocrity does not imply a value judgment, but rather a description of a certain attitude and approach to life.

From this objective perspective, we can understand that the phrase suggests that we are all destined to face the eventuality of anonymity and that those who lead a mediocre life may experience this fate earlier due to their lack of significant actions or achievements that distinguish them.

Remember that each individual has the ability to choose how to live their life and what meaning to give it. The phrase does not imply that we should settle for mediocrity, but rather invites us to reflect on the importance of seeking our own purpose and transcending the limits of a common existence.

"Literature is nothing more than a directed dream."

– Jorge Luis Borges

TO ME, BORGES invites us to understand literature as a means through which writers can shape and direct their dreams and visions. As a writer, I believe literature is a tool that allows us to explore our imagination and express our ideas in words. It is a vehicle that enables us to create worlds, characters, and situations that may seem dreamlike and surreal.

Literature, in my experience, is a form of artistic expression that goes beyond mere storytelling. It is a medium for conveying emotions, reflections, and profound concepts. Through words, I can create my own universe and guide readers through it, sharing my thoughts, concerns, and perceptions in a unique way.

In this sense, the term "directed" in Borges's phrase takes on a special meaning. Not only are we dreaming as we write, but we are also taking on the role of directors of our literary dreams. We can shape the plot, characters, tone, and atmosphere of our works according to our vision and purpose.

However, it is important to highlight that this direction does not imply absolute control. Just like in dreams, literature can also surprise us and take us down unexpected paths. Sometimes, our own characters can come to life and challenge our initial intentions. It is in these moments that the magic of writing is revealed and plunges us into new creative explorations.

As a writer, I find in literature a means to shape my dreams and share them with others. It is a creative experience that allows me to guide readers through imaginary worlds and convey my thoughts uniquely. Embracing this vision, I find in literature a powerful medium for self-expression and connecting with others on a deep and emotional level.

The phrase "Literature is nothing more than a directed dream" comes to life in the minds of those who immerse themselves in the world of words and stories. From a third-person perspective, we can delve into Borges's vision and explore how this idea manifests in the experiences of writers and readers.

In the vast literary universe, authors become the architects of their own fantasies. Like masters of ceremonies, they direct their dreams and transform them into captivating narratives. Every written word is a thread weaving a tapestry of imaginary worlds, vibrant characters, and palpable emotions.

Writers, with their pens as magic wands, breathe life into their dreams and control them with precision. They build dazzling settings, populated by extraordinary beings intertwined in intricate plots. They are the directors in this theater of imagination, guiding readers through paths of surprises and revelations.

But in the vast ocean of literature, there is also room for mystery and the unexpected. Sometimes, words take on a life of their own and veer off the path laid out by the author. Characters rebel, acquire their own voices, and defy established expectations. At that moment, the author becomes a mere witness, letting the literary dream take its own course.

And so, readers delve into this directed dream, traveling through printed pages to unknown lands. They are passengers on this literary journey, open to the experience and willing to be carried away by the current of the narrative. Every word and every twist of the plot immerse them deeper into the dream woven by the author.

In this context, literature becomes a portal that transports readers beyond their own realities. It is a means to explore different perspectives, emotions, and human dilemmas. Through reading, individuals immerse themselves in an alternate reality, where they can contemplate the world from other viewpoints and reflect on the human condition.

In conclusion, literature is a directed dream that takes shape in the hands of writers and comes to life in the imagination of readers. It is a shared journey, where authors and readers meet in a space where words transcend time and space. In that literary dream, we discover the magic of creation and the profound connection that exists between those who bring words to life and those who eagerly receive them.

> # "Only that which is gone
> is what belongs to us."
> – Jorge Luis Borges

THIS PARADOX INVITES us to reflect on the concept of ownership and the passage of time.

In my experience, I have come to understand that the only thing we truly possess is the past, that which has already happened and remains in our memory. The present is ephemeral and slips through our fingers, while the future is uncertain and subject to constant change. That is why the paradox is posed that only what has gone, that is, what has already passed and is in the past, is what truly belongs to us.

When something or someone disappears from our lives, whether due to death, distance, or the end of a stage, we realize their true value. It is in their absence that we appreciate what we had and understand their significance in our lives. Nostalgia and the feeling of loss make us value even more what is no longer present.

However, it is important to remember that although we only have access to the past, that does not mean we should live anchored to it. Life is constantly moving, and we must learn to flow with it. We appreciate what is gone, but we must also learn to live in the present and look towards the future with hope and determination.

Ultimately, the paradox invites us to reflect on the temporality and changing nature of life. It reminds us of the importance of valuing and making the most of each present moment, as it will soon become the past. Only through full awareness of our present can we build a meaningful and enriching life.

As you progress, you realize that only what you have left behind is what truly belongs to you. It is the lessons learned, the shared moments, and the emotions experienced in those past islands that have shaped and defined you up to this point in your journey. This reminds us of the importance of fully living each present experience and learning from it, as it will soon become a distant memory. It invites us to value the past without clinging to it and to be open to new islands to discover on our life journey.

Just as the ship must continue sailing towards the horizon, we too must move forward, appreciating what we have lived and learned in the past, but without losing sight of the present and the future that are still to come.

"Happiness does not need to be transmuted into beauty, but misfortune does."

– Jorge Luis Borges

HAPPINESS IS A state of mind, a feeling of fulfillment and satisfaction that lies beyond physical or aesthetic appearance.

On the other hand, misfortune, difficult moments, and painful experiences often find their expression in beauty. Adversity can be the impetus that triggers creativity and artistic transformation. Amidst sadness, melancholy, or anguish, artists can find the passion to create works that capture the depth of human experience and convey universal emotions.

Throughout history, great works of art, poetry, and music have emerged from adversity and suffering. Personal and collective tragedies have inspired artists to channel their emotions into forms that transcend pain and find expression in aesthetic beauty. Misfortune, in its transmutation through art, becomes a manifestation that allows others to understand and connect with the depth of human experience.

This paradox leads us to reflect on how happiness and misfortune, despite their apparent contrast, are intertwined in the complexity of existence. Happiness does not need to be transformed into beauty, as its essence lies in the joy and fulfillment felt internally. Meanwhile, misfortune, through its transmutation into beauty, shows us how artistic expression can arise even from the most difficult and tragic situations.

Where happiness and misfortune intertwine emerges an intriguing paradox that challenges the boundaries of understanding. Happiness, that elusive nectar that caresses the soul with its warm embrace, does not need to be metamorphosed into beauty to be experienced in all its fullness. It stands as a radiant sun, illuminating the innermost corners of being, without the need for the adorned attire of aesthetics.

However, misfortune, with its entourage of shadows and unrest, finds a different path to transmutation. When the threads of misfortune intertwine with the loom of existence, the human soul. It is in those moments of tearing and pain where the echoes of suffering reverberate in the depth of being and awaken the inner muse.

Just as a phoenix rises from its own ashes, misfortune, in its cruel paradox, nourishes man's creative spirit. Melancholic notes merge with the poet's ink, drawing verses that distill the bitter nectar of sadness, but also encapsulate the transformative power of artistic expression. In each brushstroke, in each vibrant chord, the human soul expresses its pain and, in turn, redeems it through beauty.

The lyrical tone of symphonies intertwines pain and hope, desolation and passion in a harmonious embrace. Painting, with its palette of vivid and dark colors, portrays the nuances of human suffering on canvases that transcend time. The poet's words, like fireflies in the night, illuminate the recesses of the soul, whispering universal truths intertwined with individual experience.

In this allegorical universe, the paradox is revealed clearly: happiness does not require the garland of beauty to be complete, while misfortune, in its ephemeral encounter with art, becomes the seed of creation. Like wandering souls in the vast sea of existence, we explore the boundaries of our own nature through the alloy of these seemingly opposing experiences.

Thus, poetic language invites us to delve into the labyrinth of paradox, where happiness and misfortune intertwine in a timeless dance without limits. It urges us to reflect on the intricate connection between human experience and the pursuit of beauty, revealing that, sometimes, it is in the darkest moments where the light of creation finds its most radiant splendor.

<blockquote>
"I have sometimes suspected
that the only thing without mystery
is happiness,
because it justifies itself."
– Jorge Luis Borges
</blockquote>

IN THE RECESSES of human thought rises an unanswered question that has intrigued philosophers, poets, and dreamers throughout the ages: what is happiness? Amidst the veils of uncertainty and speculation, emerges a suggestive suspicion: happiness, in its pure essence, stands as an entity exempt from mystery.

In the vastness of existence, many things astound us, sparking our curiosity and immersing us in a sea of questions. The hidden secrets in the depths of the universe, the complexities of the human mind, and the enigmas of nature invite us into an eternal game of discovery. However, amidst this tangle of mysteries, happiness seems to rise as an exception, like a radiant beacon that illuminates without the need for explanations.

Happiness presents itself to us as an incontrovertible reality, as an experience that justifies itself. It does not require rational analysis or exhaustive search for external reasons to be validated. It is a state of fulfillment and bliss that manifests in the human being directly, without the need for explanations or arguments. In its most genuine essence, happiness reveals itself as an intimate and immediate experience, free from the shackles of thought and the chains of analysis.

Perhaps it is precisely the absence of mystery that makes it even more precious. In a world where so many things seem to escape our understanding, where enigmas multiply and answers fade into the mist of ignorance, happiness presents itself as an oasis of certainty. It is a primordial force that propels us, enveloping us in its warm embrace and whispering in our ear that life, in its deepest essence, is meant to be enjoyed and celebrated.

Although it may seem paradoxical, it is precisely the lack of mystery in happiness that endows it with its transformative power. Not being subject to logic or rational explanations, happiness becomes a liberating force, a balm that soothes the wounds of the soul and renews our energies. It is a constant reminder that, despite the complexity and uncertainties of existence, joy is within our reach, waiting to be embraced.

Ultimately, the suspicion that happiness lacks mystery invites us to appreciate it in all its simplicity and spontaneity. It challenges us to free ourselves from the bonds of excessive analysis and to immerse ourselves in the flow of life with confidence and surrender. Because, after all, happiness does not need to be unraveled or explained, but simply experienced and lived in all its fullness.

"**O**ver the years I have observed
that beauty, like happiness, is frequent.
Not a day goes by when we are not,
for a moment, in paradise."
— Jorge Luis Borges

AS THE YEARS glide gently through the loom of time, I have learned to contemplate with wise and appreciative eyes the world around me. In my journey through existence, I have come to understand that beauty, like happiness, is frequently present in our lives. There is not a day that passes without us immersing ourselves, even if just for a brief moment, in paradise.

Beauty reveals itself in the rays of the sun caressing the skin at dawn, in the intoxicating perfume of a flower awakening to the morning dew, in the warm embrace of a loved one comforting our soul. Beauty is found in every corner, patiently waiting to be discovered by those who know how to look beyond the obvious.

By opening our eyes and hearts to the wonders that surround us, we realize that paradise is within our reach with every step we take. It can manifest in the melody of a song that transports us to other worlds, in the sincere smile of a stranger brightening our path, in the whisper of the wind among the trees sharing ancestral secrets. Paradise unfolds before us in multiple forms, inviting us to immerse ourselves in its grace and splendor.

Sometimes, amidst the whirlwind of life, we may forget to stop and appreciate the beauty around us. We get distracted by worries and responsibilities, letting the days fade away without seizing the opportunities that lie before us. But when we become aware and open our senses to the magic of the present, we realize that paradise is always present, patiently waiting for us to discover it.

Thus, in the course of my existence, I have understood that beauty and happiness are not distant and unattainable entities, but faithful companions walking beside us in every step of the way. They invite us to appreciate the treasures that surround us, to savor the joy of life, and to be aware that happiness is found in every moment, waiting to be embraced.

Beauty and happiness are inseparable companions in our journey through life. They remind us that, although challenges may be present, there is always the possibility of finding a glimpse of paradise in the simplest and most ordinary moments. All it takes is to open our eyes and hearts, to let ourselves be carried away by the wonder of the present, and to be privileged witnesses of the beauty that surrounds us.

"I do not speak of revenge or forgiveness, forgetting is the only revenge and the only forgiveness."

– Jorge Luis Borges

WHEN I REFER to revenge and forgiveness, I am not speaking in terms of acts of retaliation or acts of mercy. For me, forgetting becomes the only path towards true reconciliation and redemption. In this ephemeral existence, forgetting becomes the only revenge and the only forgiveness.

Forgetting is a powerful tool that allows us to free ourselves from the weight of the past and move towards a future filled with hope and renewal. By leaving behind grudges and resentments, we free ourselves from the chains that bind us to events and people who have caused us pain. By forgetting, we stop feeding the fire of resentment and allow our wounds to heal and transform into wisdom.

Revenge, in its essence, only perpetuates an endless cycle of pain and suffering. By seeking retaliation, we plunge into a downward spiral of resentment and violence that only distances us from inner peace and harmony with our surroundings. Instead, by choosing to forget, we break free from that destructive cycle and open ourselves to the possibility of healing our wounds and finding inner peace.

Forgiveness, on the other hand, can be a complex and difficult concept to attain. However, sometimes forgiveness lies in the act of letting go, in releasing ourselves from the emotional burden of holding onto the faults and mistakes of others. By forgiving, we do not justify harmful actions or forget the lessons learned, but we allow ourselves to let go of resentment and find peace within our hearts.

Ultimately, forgetting becomes revenge and forgiveness because it gives us the opportunity to start anew. It allows us to close painful chapters and open our minds and hearts to new experiences and relationships.

Forgetting frees us from the past and propels us forward, where we can build a life based on understanding, compassion, and growth.

So, in my view of things, I do not speak of revenge or forgiveness in their traditional sense. Instead, I invite embracing the transformative power of forgetting, which gives us the opportunity to free ourselves from the past and find peace and fulfillment in the present. In forgetting lies revenge against past grievances and forgiveness towards ourselves and others.

By letting go of resentment and wounds, forgetting becomes a revenge against the past, a form of emancipation from the chains that bind us to past grievances. But at the same time, forgetting also becomes a liberating forgiveness. Through its erasing power, it allows scars to fade and wounds to heal. It is in this act of forgetting that we find reconciliation with ourselves and with others.

In this game of contradictions, I discover the paradoxical beauty of forgetting as revenge and forgiveness. It teaches us that life is full of nuances and that opposites can coexist in perfect harmony. Instead of seeking a single answer, it invites us to explore the mysteries of our own humanity.

Thus, in the duality of forgetting as revenge and forgiveness, we find a powerful expression of our emotional complexity. It is an oxymoron that invites us to reflect on our actions, our emotions, and our capacity for transformation. In the paradox of this phrase lies the challenge and beauty of our personal journey towards redemption and inner peace.

May in this dance of contradictions, we find the strength to forgive and free ourselves from the past, and in that forgetting, discover a transformative revenge that leads us to peace and fulfillment."

"Tyrannies foster stupidity."

– Jorge Luis Borges

WHEN TYRANNIES EXERCISE their oppressive power over a people, they create an environment conducive to the proliferation of stupidity. This phenomenon is due to various factors that are intrinsically linked to the exercise of authoritarian power.

Firstly, tyrannies tend to suppress freedom of thought and expression. They impose strict control over information and promote a one-dimensional view of reality. This limits people's ability to question, analyze, and form their own opinions, thereby contributing to the proliferation of simplistic and unfounded ideas.

Additionally, tyrannies foster a cult of blind obedience and submission. Absolute loyalty to the leader or regime is demanded, without allowing for discrepancies or critical thinking. This mentality of following without questioning contributes to conformity and uncritical acceptance of ideas imposed by the tyranny, even when they lack logical or rational foundation.

Another important factor is fear. Tyrannies often create a climate of constant fear, where reprisals and consequences for expressing contrary opinions are severe. This fear inhibits intellectual development and promotes conformity out of fear of reprisals, leading people to adopt a passive and resigned stance, distancing them from the pursuit of knowledge and the confrontation of ideas.

In summary, tyrannies foster stupidity by limiting freedom of thought, promoting uncritical submission, and generating a climate of fear that inhibits intellectual development. In this context, simplistic and unfounded ideas prevail, making it difficult for a critical and conscious society to emerge.

"Do not speak unless you can improve upon the silence."

– Jorge Luis Borges

THIS STATEMENT IMPLIES recognizing that silence can be more eloquent and powerful than empty or superfluous words. Silence can convey peace, wisdom, and serenity, while inappropriate or unnecessary words can create noise, discord, or misunderstandings.

To put it into practice, it is important to develop a greater awareness of our words and evaluate whether they truly improve upon the silence. Before speaking, we should consider whether our words will be constructive, inspiring, or beneficial for those who hear us and for ourselves.

A practical example would be in a meeting or debate, where a person refrains from intervening unless they have a solid argument or relevant idea to contribute. Instead of filling the space with empty words or unsubstantial comments, this person chooses to listen carefully to others, reflect on what has been said, and when they truly have something valuable to offer, speak clearly and precisely, thus enhancing the silence that preceded them.

Through the practice of reflective silence and the careful selection of our expressions, we can contribute to an environment of greater harmony and significance, where our words truly have a positive and enriching impact.

"In my next life,
I will try to make more mistakes."

– Jorge Luis Borges

THROUGHOUT MY EXISTENCE, I have come to understand that making mistakes is not synonymous with absolute failure, but rather an opportunity to learn, evolve, and improve. Each mistake made is like a stone on the path of my life, a stone that I can pick up, examine, and turn into a stepping stone towards wisdom and maturity.

In my next life, I pledge not to fear mistakes but to embrace them as valuable companions on my journey. I will awaken each day with the determination to live fully, making mistakes and learning from them. I will be like a fearless navigator, exploring new horizons and facing challenges with courage and humility. Each mistake will be another step in my journey towards self-realization and inner wisdom.

In my next life, I have come to the conclusion that I will try to make more mistakes. It may seem contradictory, as we generally associate mistakes with failures or negative situations. However, I have learned that mistakes are valuable opportunities for growth and learning.

When I say I will try to make more mistakes, I do not mean to deliberately seek failure or act negligently. What I mean is that I want to be braver and more daring in my choices and actions. I want to dare to step out of my comfort zone, explore new horizons, and challenge the limits imposed by fear and insecurity.

Imagine life as a path full of trails. Every time we make a mistake, it's like taking an unexpected detour. It may seem confusing or even frustrating at that moment, but it is in those moments of deviation where we find the most valuable lessons and discover parts of ourselves that we may not have known.

Think of a navigator venturing into a vast ocean. If they stick to their comfort zone and cling to familiar routes, they will never discover new lands or exciting experiences. But if they allow themselves to make mistakes by choosing wrong directions or facing unexpected storms, they will open the doors to a world of endless possibilities.

That's how I see my next life. I want to be that fearless navigator, willing to risk getting lost to find hidden treasures. I want to embrace every mistake as an opportunity for growth and a lesson that brings me closer to the person I want to be.

In summary, in my next life, I long to make more mistakes because I know that in them, I will find the spark of growth and transformation. Like the navigator venturing into the ocean, I am willing to lose myself along the way to find myself and discover all that the journey has in store for me.

> ## "From my weakness,
> ## I gained a strength
> ## that never abandoned me."
>
> – Jorge Luis Borges

THIS PHRASE ENCAPSULATES a profound reflection on the human capacity to turn difficulties into strengths. In this statement, it is acknowledged that even in our most vulnerable and fragile moments, we can find an inner strength that propels and sustains us throughout our lives.

The weakness referred to is not limited solely to physical limitations but encompasses all forms of fragility, whether emotional, mental, or spiritual. It is in those moments of vulnerability where we discover our true nature and our ability to confront and overcome challenges.

When we find ourselves in a state of weakness, we are often compelled to confront our limitations and seek ways to overcome them. It is in this process of self-discovery and personal growth that we find the inner strength that never abandons us. This strength does not arise from denying our weaknesses but from accepting and transforming them.

By embracing our weaknesses and learning from them, we develop a resilience that strengthens us in all aspects of our lives. We learn to find the courage and determination to face obstacles, and we become more compassionate and empathetic beings towards ourselves and others.

Through the acceptance and learning from our weaknesses, we can find a lasting inner strength that propels us to grow, overcome challenges, and live a more fulfilling and meaningful life.

"The truth never penetrates an unwilling mind."

– Jorge Luis Borges

OPENNESS AND WILLINGNESS are essential for seeking and accepting truth. If our minds are closed or unreceptive, truth remains hidden and inaccessible.

Truth refers to objective reality, to the deeper understanding of things as they are. However, this understanding can only take place if we are willing to question our preconceived beliefs, to examine our ideas, and to open ourselves to new perspectives.

When our mind is closed, rooted in prejudices, or trapped in rigid dogmas, it is difficult for the truth to penetrate it. We cling to our pre-existing ideas and filter information according to our own beliefs, which can distort our perception of reality.

For truth to find a place in our mind, we must be willing to question our own assumptions, to listen to different viewpoints, and to examine evidence impartially. This requires intellectual humility, the ability to recognize our own limitations, and the willingness to learn and grow.

A practical example of this statement can be found in the scientific field. Scientists are constantly seeking truth through research and rigorous analysis. However, if a scientist stubbornly clings to an established theory and is unwilling to consider new evidence or perspectives, they are unlikely to discover the most complete or accurate truth. Only those scientists who maintain an open mind and are willing to challenge their own preconceived ideas can advance in the understanding of scientific truth.

In summary, the phrase "The truth never penetrates an unwilling mind" urges us to cultivate mental openness and willingness to question our beliefs and explore different perspectives. Only through this attitude of humility and curiosity can we open ourselves to the discovery and understanding of truth.

"Poets, like the blind, can see in the darkness."

– Jorge Luis Borges

THIS PHRASE EVOKES a profound connection between poets and their ability to perceive and express beauty even in the darkest moments.

For me, poetry is a means of exploring the depths of the human being and capturing the essence of human experiences in words. Poets have a special sensitivity, a keen insight that allows them to see beyond superficial appearances and penetrate to the essence of things.

When it is mentioned that poets can see in the darkness, it refers to their ability to find beauty and meaning even in the most challenging and difficult moments of life. While others may feel overwhelmed by darkness, poets find inspiration in it and are able to reveal hidden and profound aspects that might otherwise go unnoticed.

Through poetry, my vision expands beyond the superficial and the obvious, delving into the depths of human experience, into the subtle nuances of emotions and feelings.

Like the blind, poets have a unique sensory perception. Although they may not be able to physically see, their internal vision is vivid and penetrating. They use words as their language and tool to paint images in the minds of readers, awakening emotions and conveying a deeper understanding of reality.

Through metaphors and evocative language, the poet is able to convey a deep and sensitive understanding of inner experiences, pointing towards our innermost selves.

In my own experience, I have felt the magic of poetry in finding beauty and meaning in moments of darkness and difficulty. It is in those moments when inspiration flows most intensely and words acquire transformative power. Through poetry, I can illuminate the darkest corners of my soul and find a profound connection with others.

Through your inner vision and poetic expression, you can allow yourself to appreciate beauty in all its forms, even in the most challenging moments of life.

5
David Bohm

About David Bohm

David Bohm's philosophy towards life and society centered on the importance of wholeness and the interconnectedness of all things. He believed in the existence of an underlying and holistic order in the universe, in contrast to a fragmented and reductionist view of reality.

Bohm maintained that fragmentation and division are the fundamental causes of problems in society. He identified the fragmentation of human thought as a barrier to understanding the totality of existence. In his work, he argued that our way of thinking is conditioned by culture, education, and experience, leading to the creation of artificial divisions between people, ideas, and systems.

Bohm advocated for a dialogical approach in communication and the pursuit of mutual understanding. He believed that authentic dialogue and attentive listening could help overcome fragmentation and promote greater coherence and harmony in society. For him, true communication involved being open to new perspectives and questioning our assumptions and entrenched beliefs.

Regarding life, Bohm advocated for a vision of existence in which we do not artificially separate nature, human beings, and the cosmos. He believed in the importance of understanding our interconnectedness with everything around us and the need to live in harmony with nature and respect it.

In summary, David Bohm's philosophy towards life and society was based on the idea of wholeness and interconnectedness. He advocated for overcoming fragmentation and promoting authentic dialogue and mutual understanding. He believed in the importance of living in harmony with nature and recognizing our interdependence with the surrounding world.

David Bohm had criticisms towards formal education and its impact on individual creativity. He considered that the traditional education system emphasized to a large extent learning based on memorization and repetition of information, which limited students' ability to develop their creative and original thinking.

Bohm argued that formal education tends to promote the fragmentation of knowledge by dividing disciplines into separate compartments. This fragmentation, according to him, inhibits deep understanding and the ability to establish meaningful connections between different areas of knowledge. Instead of fostering a holistic and coherent view of the world, formal education often creates stagnant compartments of knowledge that hinder the complete understanding of phenomena.

Regarding individual creativity, Bohm considered that traditional education often restricts creative expression and limits students' ability to think independently. He believed that creative thinking is hindered by the emphasis on conformity and uniformity in the education system, which rewards "correct" answers and discourages the exploration of new ideas and approaches.

Bohm advocated for an educational approach that promotes freedom of thought and the ability to ask meaningful questions. He believed that creativity and originality are fundamental elements in solving complex problems and advancing society. He defended the importance of cultivating curiosity, critical thinking, and the ability to explore multiple perspectives to foster creativity in individuals.

David Bohm had a critical view of formal education and its impact on individual creativity. He considered that the traditional education system fostered fragmented thinking and limited people's creative capacity.

Bohm argued that conventional education mainly emphasized the development of analytical skills and accumulative knowledge, leading to a fragmented and narrow way of thinking. According to him, this approach restricted the ability to see connections and holistic relationships between ideas and phenomena.

Instead of promoting creativity and the exploration of new possibilities, Bohm believed that formal education tended to focus on the reproduction of knowledge and conformity to established norms. He believed that this limited people's ability to think originally and develop new and fresh ideas.

Bohm advocated for the importance of fostering creativity in education, encouraging students to question, explore, and discover for themselves. He considered creativity essential for addressing the complex and emerging challenges of society and for finding innovative solutions.

Furthermore, Bohm argued that creativity was not limited only to artistic areas but was a fundamental capacity in all aspects of life. He saw creativity as an expression of the mind in action and believed that by fostering it, a greater understanding and capacity for personal and social transformation could be cultivated.

In conclusion, David Bohm viewed formal education as an obstacle to individual creativity due to its emphasis on fragmented thinking and conformity. He advocated for an educational approach that promoted exploration, questioning, and the ability to think holistically, recognizing the importance of creativity in all aspects of life.

Wisdom Quotes by David Bohm

"THE REAL DIALOGUE OCCURS
WHEN TWO OR MORE PEOPLE
ARE WILLING TO SUSPEND THEIR CERTAINTY
IN THE PRESENCE OF THE OTHER."

"Thought controls you.
However, thought gives false information
that you are controlling it.
In reality, it is thought that controls each one of us."

"THE ABILITY TO PERCEIVE OR THINK DIFFERENTLY
IS MORE IMPORTANT THAN ACQUIRED KNOWLEDGE."

"TO CHANGE YOUR REALITY,
YOU MUST CHANGE YOUR INTERNAL THOUGHTS."

"SPACE IS NOT EMPTY.
IT IS FULL A PLENITUDE INSTEAD OF A VOID
AND IT IS THE FOUNDATION
OF THE EXISTENCE OF EVERYTHING
INCLUDING OURSELVES.
THE UNIVERSE IS NOT SEPARATE
FROM THIS COSMIC SEA OF ENERGY."

"INDIVIDUALITY IS ONLY POSSIBLE
IF IT DEVELOPS FROM WHOLENESS."

"WE ARE ALL CONNECTED BY A NETWORK
OF INVISIBLE CONNECTIONS.
THIS NETWORK IS CONSTANTLY CHANGING AND EVOLVING.
THIS FIELD IS STRUCTURED AND DIRECTLY INFLUENCED
BY OUR BEHAVIOR AND UNDERSTANDING.

"AT A DEEP LEVEL, HUMANITY'S CONSCIOUSNESS IS ONE.
THIS IS PRACTICALLY CERTAIN
BECAUSE EVEN IN EMPTINESS, MATTER IS ONE;
AND IF WE DO NOT SEE THIS,
IT IS BECAUSE WE ARE BLINDING OURSELVES TO IT."

"What is needed is to learn again,
observe, and discover for ourselves
the meaning of wholeness."

"ULTIMATELY, ALL MOMENTS ARE TRULY ONE,
THEREFORE, THE NOW IS AN ETERNITY."

"IN THE LONG RUN IT IS MUCH MORE DANGEROUS
TO CLING TO ILLUSION THAN TO FACE
WHAT THE ACTUAL FACT IS.
"

"If we can delight in positive images,
we can also become depressed with negative ones.
While we accept images as realities,
we become trapped because we cannot control the images."

"WE COULD SAY THAT PRACTICALLY ALL THE PROBLEMS
OF THE HUMAN RACE STEM FROM THE FACT
THAT THOUGHT IS NOT PROPRIOCEPTIVE."

"In nature, nothing remains constant.
Everything is in a perpetual state
of transformation, movement, and change."

My Commentary on
David Bohm
Quotes

"**The real dialogue occurs
when two or more people
are willing to suspend their certainty
in the presence of the other.**"
– David Bohm

THIS PHRASE CAPTURES the essence of authentic and meaningful communication, where the exchange of ideas and perspectives takes place in an atmosphere of openness and willingness to question our own beliefs.

The most enriching and constructive dialogue happens when I set aside my need to always be right and am willing to truly listen to others. This entails putting aside my own certainties and prejudices, and being open to considering different viewpoints and approaches.

When I enter into dialogue with an attitude of humility and openness, I can learn and grow through interaction with others. By suspending my certainty, I am willing to question my own ideas and explore new perspectives. This does not mean abandoning my values or fundamental principles, but rather opening myself to the possibility of expanding my understanding and knowledge.

When participants are willing to suspend their certainty and actively listen to others, a space is created where different arguments can be examined and stronger conclusions reached. In contrast, if everyone rigidly maintains their position and refuses to consider other viewpoints, dialogue becomes a clash of opinions without true progress.

Real and meaningful dialogue requires the willingness to suspend our certainty and listen with an open mind. By doing so, we can explore new ideas, better understand others, and find more creative and collaborative solutions. Authentic dialogue invites us into a space of mutual learning and personal growth, where connection and understanding are strengthened.

"Thought controls you.
However, thought gives false information
that you are controlling it.
In reality, it is thought that controls each one of us."

– David Bohm

WE OFTEN BELIEVE that we are the owners and controllers of our thoughts, but in reality, we are immersed in a constant flow of ideas, beliefs, and judgments that condition us and deeply influence us.

Thought can be deceptive, as it gives us the illusion that we are in control when in reality we are being controlled by it. We cling to our preconceived ideas, to our subjective interpretations of reality, and to our habitual thought patterns. These patterns can limit our understanding and our ability to see beyond our own perspectives.

A practical example of this dynamic is found in moments when we find ourselves trapped in negative or self-destructive thoughts. We may believe that we are controlling those thoughts, but in reality, they are controlling us, generating negative emotions and affecting our perception of ourselves and the world around us.

To free ourselves from the oppressive influence of thought, it is important to cultivate awareness and non-judgmental observation. By recognizing that we are more than our thoughts and that we can examine them from a more objective perspective, we can begin to free ourselves from their control. The practice of mindfulness and meditation helps us develop this ability to observe our thoughts without identifying with them.

By becoming aware of how thought controls us, we can begin to question its limiting narratives and open ourselves to new ways of thinking and perceiving. This allows us to explore reality more clearly and free ourselves from the mental bonds that prevent us from experiencing a fuller and more authentic life.

Thought has a powerful influence on us, but it often deceives us by making us believe that we are the controllers. By recognizing this dynamic and developing greater awareness of our thoughts, we can free ourselves from their control and open ourselves to new possibilities of perception and experience.

"The ability to perceive or think differently is more important than acquired knowledge."

– David Bohm

THIS STATEMENT EMPHASIZES the importance of mental flexibility and openness to new ideas and perspectives, as opposed to simply accumulating information and knowledge without questioning it or putting it into context.

From my point of view, this idea highlights the importance of cultivating the mind and developing critical thinking skills. If we limit ourselves to acquiring knowledge without questioning it or seeking new ways of thinking, we run the risk of becoming stuck in a single view of the world.

A practical example of this premise can be found in the scientific field. Throughout history, scientific advances have emerged from researchers' ability to question established theories and explore new possibilities. If scientists had settled for existing knowledge and had not been willing to think differently, many important discoveries would not have been possible.

Furthermore, the ability to perceive or think differently fosters creativity and innovation. In art, for example, those who dare to explore new forms of expression or challenge established conventions often generate original and provocative works.

Similarly, in the social and cultural sphere, the ability to perceive or think differently allows for greater understanding and respect for individual and cultural differences. By being open to different viewpoints, we can enrich our understanding of the world and promote constructive dialogue.

In conclusion, the ability to perceive or think differently is essential for our personal and collective growth. It allows us to overcome intellectual complacency, question established ideas, and explore new possibilities. By fostering mental flexibility and openness to diverse thinking, we can broaden our horizons and contribute to the progress and development of society.

TO CHANGE YOUR reality, you must change your internal thoughts. This statement highlights the importance of the connection between the mind and people's life experiences. It recognizes that our perceptions and thoughts influence how we experience the world and how we relate to it.

In this sense, if we wish to transform our reality, we must start by examining and modifying our thought patterns. If we continue to cling to limiting beliefs, fears, or negative thoughts, we are likely to continue experiencing similar circumstances and feel stuck.

By changing our internal thoughts, we can change our perspective and focus, which in turn affects our actions and decisions. If we cultivate positive, optimistic, and empowering thoughts, we are more likely to attract experiences and opportunities aligned with that mindset.

People who have achieved significant changes in their lives have often worked on transforming their limiting thoughts and adopting a growth mindset. By changing their internal narrative and focusing on thoughts of abundance, overcoming, and possibilities, they have managed to break barriers and achieve goals that once seemed unattainable.

Likewise, in the field of psychology, it is recognized that recurrent negative thoughts can contribute to self-destructive or unhealthy behavior patterns. By addressing and modifying those thoughts, positive changes can be generated in how people perceive themselves, interact with others, and face life's challenges.

To change your reality, it is necessary for each individual to discover their own limitation, since the very act of realizing those limits can generate understanding and open a new scenario where change flourishes.

"Space is not empty.
It is full, a plenitude instead of a void,
and it is the foundation of the existence of everything,
including ourselves.
The universe is not separate
from this cosmic sea of energy."

– David Bohm

WHEN WE TALK about "space," we refer to the vastness that surrounds us, the universe in which we dwell. Often, we have tended to consider it as mere emptiness, an absence of material objects. However, from a deeper perspective, it is argued that space is composed of an intricate network of energy, vibrations, and quantum fields that interconnect everything in the universe.

The idea that space is filled implies that there is no separation between us and the universe. We are an integral part of this cosmic fullness of energy. Our very existence is intertwined with the energetic fabric of space. Instead of being isolated entities, we are interdependent and connected to everything around us.

This understanding has profound implications in various fields of study. In quantum physics, for example, it has been discovered that subatomic particles emerge from the quantum field, which permeates all space. In spirituality and Eastern philosophy, it is taught that everything in the universe is a manifestation of interconnected universal consciousness.

Recognize that we are immersed in a cosmic sea of interconnected energy. This understanding can awaken a greater appreciation of our existence and a sense of unity with the world around us."

"Individuality is only possible if it is developed from wholeness."

– David Bohm

DAVID BOHM PROPOSED the idea that true individuality can only arise if it is developed from wholeness. This assertion suggests that our true essence as individuals is not found in separation and fragmentation, but in our connection and belonging to a larger whole.

According to Bohm, wholeness refers to the underlying unity that encompasses the entire universe, a wholeness that transcends apparent divisions. Instead of seeing ourselves as separate and independent entities, Bohm suggests that our authentic individuality lies in our conscious participation in wholeness and our ability to perceive and act from that broader perspective.

From this viewpoint, the development of individuality involves a profound understanding and connection with the environment in which we live. It is not about selfishly asserting our own uniqueness, but about recognizing that our individuality is nurtured and strengthened by acknowledging and honoring our interdependence with other beings and the environment.

A practical example of this idea can be found in the realm of creativity. When a person engages in a creative process, such as writing, painting, or composing music, their individuality is expressed through their unique expression. However, this individuality does not arise in isolation but is nourished by influences and connections with the surrounding world. Experiences, interactions with others, observation of nature, and access to various forms of knowledge enrich and shape individual expression.

In summary, David Bohm's assertion that individuality is only possible if developed from wholeness invites us to transcend the illusion of separation and recognize our interconnectedness with the world. By developing our individuality from this broader perspective, we can achieve a greater sense of authenticity and contribute significantly to the well-being of the whole.

"We are all connected by a network of invisible connections. This network is constantly changing and evolving. This field is structured and directly influenced by our behavior and understanding."

– David Bohm

WE ARE ALL immersed in a network of invisible connections that binds us all, both at the human level and with the environment in which we live. This network is dynamic and constantly evolving, adapting to our interactions and experiences.

Every thought, every action, and every choice we make has an impact on this human network. Our behavior and understanding are fundamental elements that shape and structure this network of connections. Each person, every living being, and every part of the universe contributes in some way to the configuration of this constantly changing network.

It is important to remember that this network is not limited only to our interpersonal relationships but encompasses the entire ecosystem in which we are immersed. Our behavior and understanding directly affect the health of the planet and all forms of life that inhabit it.

Ultimately, by being aware of our interconnectedness with this invisible network, we can make more informed and responsible decisions. Understanding that our actions have an impact on others and the environment invites us to act with greater care and consideration.

This network is dynamic and constantly evolving, and each of us has the ability to positively influence it through our actions and conscious choices. By recognizing and honoring this interconnection, we can contribute to the harmony and well-being of all beings and the planet as a whole.

David Bohm sought to highlight the idea that, despite our apparent individuality and separation, we are intrinsically connected to one another and to the universe as a whole. His assertion about the existence of a network of invisible connections suggests that there is a fundamental interdependence in the fabric of reality.

Bohm emphasized that this network is not static but constantly changing and evolving. He implied that our actions, thoughts, and understanding have a direct impact on this network and therefore on the environment around us. Our way of relating to the world and others influences the structure and flow of these invisible connections.

By highlighting the influence of our behavior and understanding on this network, Bohm invited us to be aware of our responsibility in creating and transforming the environment in which we live. He urged us to cultivate a greater awareness of how our actions and thoughts can affect others and the world at large.

DEEP DOWN, I feel that humanity's consciousness is one. Although sometimes we perceive ourselves as separate individual beings, there is an underlying connection that binds us all. This connection is reflected in the interdependence of matter in the universe.

When I observe the world around me, I recognize that everything is composed of the same fundamental elements. The same energy and matter that constitute me are also present in all things. It's as if we are different manifestations of the same underlying reality.

However, sometimes I blind myself to this truth. I get distracted by the superficial appearances of separation and individuality. I forget about the profound unity that binds us all. It's important to remember that even in apparent emptiness, matter is united.

This understanding invites me to open my eyes and see beyond the illusions of separation. It challenges me to recognize and embrace the interconnectedness that exists at every level: from human relationships to our relationship with nature and the universe as a whole.

Realizing this underlying unity, I feel called to act from a place of compassion and care towards others and the environment. I recognize that my actions have an impact on the whole, and that my choices can contribute to harmony and balance.

This understanding invites me to expand my consciousness and transcend the limitations of a fragmented view of the world. It encourages me to seek unity amidst diversity and to recognize the profound interconnectedness that binds us as human beings.

"**W**hat is needed is to learn again,
observe, and discover for ourselves
the meaning of wholeness."

– David Bohm

THE PHRASE "WHAT is needed is to learn anew, to observe, and to discover for ourselves the meaning of wholeness" emphasizes the importance of abandoning preconceived ideas and notions imposed by others to open ourselves to a direct and personal understanding of the entirety of life.

Krishnamurti and Bohm, in their dialogues, emphasized the need to question and deeply examine our ingrained beliefs and cultural conditioning. They urged us to free ourselves from external influences and embark on an inner journey of exploration to discover the truth for ourselves.

Learning anew involves unlearning, setting aside mental patterns and preconceived ideas that limit us and prevent us from seeing the entirety of existence. It is an act of humility and openness to new perspectives, allowing us to discover truth beyond conceptual and mental limitations.

Observing is fundamental in this process. Krishnamurti and Bohm encouraged us to observe without judgment or interpretation, simply seeing things as they are, without the interference of conditioned mind. Through this impartial observation, we can gain a deeper and more direct understanding of reality.

Discovering for ourselves entails autonomy and responsibility to seek our own truth. Krishnamurti and Bohm emphasized that truth cannot be transmitted or taught but must be realized and experienced individually. Only through our own exploration and discovery can we grasp the complete meaning of wholeness.

In summary, this phrase invites us to relinquish dependence on external authorities and engage in a process of self-inquiry and self-discovery. It urges us to question and free ourselves from mental conditioning to open ourselves to a direct perception of the entirety of life. Only by learning anew, observing attentively, and discovering for ourselves can we approach the deepest truth and experience genuine transformation in our understanding and relationship with the world.

"Ultimately, all moments are truly one, therefore, the now is an eternity."

– David Bohm

WHEN IT IS mentioned that "ultimately, all moments are truly one," it is referring to the idea that linear time is a construct of our minds and that, on a deeper level, all moments exist simultaneously.

According to this perspective, the past, present, and future are not separate entities but are interconnected and part of an indivisible whole. Each moment we experience intertwines with the others, creating a network of interdependence and unity.

In relation to the assertion that "the now is an eternity," it is pointing out that the present is the only point in time where we can experience and have direct awareness. It is in the present moment where our existence unfolds and where we have the ability to experience the fullness of life.

From this perspective, the now is considered as a timeless state of consciousness, in which the experience of reality is revealed in its entirety. It is a state in which the limitations of linear time dissolve and access to a sense of eternity is gained, where each moment contains an infinite richness of possibilities and experiences.

The phrase "ultimately, all moments are truly one, therefore, the now is an eternity" invites us to transcend our limited perception of time and recognize the unity and continuity in all experience. It reminds us that each present moment contains infinite depth and invites us to immerse ourselves in the present with full awareness and openness, acknowledging the vastness and eternity unfolding in each instant.

"In the long run, it is much more dangerous to cling to illusion than to face what the actual fact is."

– David Bohm

AT TIMES, WE may find ourselves trapped in illusions or fantasies that provide us with a sense of comfort, security, or escape from uncomfortable situations. However, if we hold onto those illusions in the long term, we may lose touch with the truth and the actual circumstances surrounding us.

Instead of avoiding or denying facts, facing reality allows us to gain a more accurate understanding of our lives and make informed decisions. By confronting the actual facts, we open ourselves up to the possibility of personal growth, learning, and transformation. Although facing reality can be challenging or even painful at times, it is essential for our long-term well-being.

By avoiding facing reality and persisting in illusion, we run the risk of perpetuating harmful situations, maintaining unsatisfactory relationships, or basing our decisions on false premises. Instead, by confronting reality, we can take steps to change negative circumstances, seek solutions, and live a more authentic and fulfilling life.

In summary, the phrase urges us to resist the temptation to cling to illusions and instead confront the actual facts. By doing so, we position ourselves more effectively to address life's challenges, make informed decisions, and live more authentically and satisfactorily in the long term.

THE PHRASE SUGGESTS that if we allow ourselves to experience joy or happiness through positive images or mental representations, we can also fall into sadness or depression when we identify with negative images. By accepting these images as absolute realities, we become prisoners of them, as we have no total control over the images and how they emotionally affect us.

The images referred to are not just visual, but also mental representations and ideas that we construct in our minds. Often, our emotions and moods are influenced by the internal images we generate and cling to.

If we attach ourselves to positive images and take them as absolute truths, we risk falling into disappointment or sadness when those images do not materialize or change. Similarly, if we identify with negative images, we can experience a depressive or hopeless state of mind.

The implicit message in the phrase is that we must be aware that the images we create in our minds are only representations and not reality itself. By recognizing that images are mental constructs and not immutable facts, we can free ourselves from their control over our emotions. In doing so, we open the door to greater emotional freedom and the ability to manage our responses more consciously and balanced.

Ultimately, the key is not to fully identify with the images and not allow them to dictate our happiness or well-being. Through the practice of mindfulness and observation of our thoughts and mental images, we can cultivate greater freedom and detach from their influence to experience greater inner peace and emotional balance.

In my personal experience, I have come to understand that if I allow myself to rejoice in positive images, I can also fall into sadness or despair when I cling to negative images. It is a constant reminder that images, whether positive or negative, are just constructs of the mind and not absolute reality.

When I identify too much with these images and take them as irrefutable truths, I find myself trapped in a cycle of fluctuating emotions and moods. I have always had a tendency to cling to positive images and reject or fear negative ones. However, over time, I have learned that this attachment to images only limits me and prevents me from seeing the totality of reality.

As I have cultivated awareness that images are just mental constructs, I have gradually been able to free myself from their control. I have learned to recognize that images do not define who I am or dictate my happiness or well-being. Instead, I have focused on exploring and understanding reality as it presents itself, without getting caught up in the illusions and projections of the mind.

By accepting that images are ephemeral and that reality transcends any mental representation, I have found greater inner peace and a sense of liberation. I have realized that clinging to images only causes me suffering and limits my perspective.

Therefore, I strive to constantly remember that images are just tools of the mind and that I should not allow them to control me. By staying open and receptive to reality as it is, I can embrace the fullness of the present moment and live with greater authenticity and freedom.

"We could say that practically all the problems of the human race stem from the fact that thought is not proprioceptive."

– David Bohm

THIS STATEMENT SUGGESTS that much of the issues humanity faces are related to the lack of self-awareness of thought. In other words, we are not aware of how our own thoughts and feelings work, or how they affect our actions and perceptions.

When it's mentioned that thought is not proprioceptive, it refers to the lack of internal awareness and deep understanding of how our own ideas, beliefs, and thought patterns influence our reality and interactions with others. We are not fully aware of how our subjective interpretations and biases can distort our view of the world and affect our decisions and behaviors.

This lack of proprioception regarding thought activity can lead to conflicts, misunderstandings, and problems on an individual and collective level. If we are not aware of our own mental tendencies and how they shape our actions, we are more likely to follow limiting thought patterns, ingrained prejudices, and destructive behaviors.

To address this issue, it is necessary to cultivate the ability of introspection and self-observation. We must be willing to question our own ideas and beliefs, to critically examine our thoughts, and to be aware of how these internal influences affect our interactions with others and the world around us.

When we develop proprioception, we can become more aware of our own limitations and biases, and open ourselves to new perspectives and ways of thinking. This allows us to find more creative solutions, better understand others, and promote harmony and cooperation in our social interactions.

In summary, the lack of proprioception of thought contributes to many of the problems we face as a species. By becoming aware of our own mental processes and being more reflective in our actions, we can work towards more effective solutions and foster a more harmonious and empathetic coexistence.

Proprioception and interoception are two important aspects of our bodily awareness and how we perceive and relate to our internal and external environment.

Proprioception refers to the ability to perceive the position, movement, and orientation of our own body in space, and this also encompasses our mind and thoughts. It is the sense that allows us to be aware of where our limbs are, the position of our joints, and the muscle tension we are experiencing. Proprioception helps us perform coordinated and precise movements, and allows us to adapt to different physical situations.

On the other hand, interoception refers to the ability to perceive internal sensations of the body, such as hunger, thirst, heart rate, breathing, and visceral sensations. Interoception provides us with information about our internal state, both physical and emotional. It allows us to recognize and respond to signals from our body, such as satiety, discomfort, or stress.

Both aspects are fundamental to maintaining real balance and overall well-being.

It is true that in our current society, we rely heavily on external information and objective data to make decisions and understand the world around us. This excessive reliance on external information can create internal conflicts, as we often ignore or underestimate our interoceptive capabilities, such as intuition, internal wisdom, and connection with our emotions and internal needs.

By primarily relying on external information, we risk disconnecting from our own experience and not tuning in to our true needs and desires. This can lead to a sense of dissatisfaction or internal conflict, as our actions and decisions may not align with our true nature.

When we underestimate our interoceptive capabilities, we miss the opportunity to leverage our internal wisdom and make decisions more aligned with our authentic self. This can create a imbalance between what we believe we "should" do based on external information and what we truly need and desire at a deeper level.

To address these internal conflicts, it is important to cultivate greater awareness of our interoceptive capabilities and learn to listen to and trust our internal wisdom. This involves dedicating time to self-reflection, mindfulness, and actively listening to our emotions and internal needs. By balancing external information with our interoceptive capabilities, we can make more authentic decisions and find greater internal harmony.

By developing greater proprioception and interoception, we can improve our ability to self-regulate, make informed decisions about our health and well-being, and cultivate a greater connection between mind and body. These skills can also be helpful in stress management, emotional regulation, and self-care.

It is important to note that both proprioception and interoception can be cultivated and improved through practices such as mindfulness, mindful movement, meditation, and body awareness training. By paying attention to our physical and emotional sensations, we can develop greater awareness and understanding of ourselves, thus promoting a better quality of life and overall well-being.

Dear Reader,

Throughout these pages, we have encountered the thoughts and reflections of some of the greatest minds in literature and art: Albert Einstein, Charles Chaplin, Mark Twain, Jorge Luis Borges, Pablo Picasso, Charles Bukowski, and David Bohm. Their words have the power to move us, challenge us, and remind us of the beauty and complexity of the human experience. I hope that in reading these quotes, you've found moments of insight, comfort, and perhaps even a spark of inspiration to carry with you.

I want to extend my deepest gratitude to you for accompanying me on this journey. Your presence has turned this book from a simple collection of words into a shared experience, rich with meaning and emotion. It is your engagement and reflection that give life to these quotes and allow them to continue to inspire.

As we part ways for now, remember that the wisdom contained within these pages is always available to you. Let these quotes serve as a beacon of light in moments of darkness, a source of strength in times of challenge, and a reminder of the enduring power of the written word.

Until we meet again, keep seeking the wisdom that lies in the words of others, and never stop exploring the boundless landscape of your own thoughts and creativity.

With heartfelt gratitude,

Paul Coty

9 798328 991445